Date: 10/5/15

J BIO MANDELA
Dakers, Diane.
Nelson Mandela : South
Africa's anti- apartheid

Nelson Mandela

SOUTH AFRICA'S
ANTI-APARTHEID REVOLUTIONARY

By Diane Dakers

Crabtree Publishing Company
www.crabtreebooks.com

Crabtree Publishing Company

www.crabtreebooks.com

Author: Diane Dakers
Publishing plan research and development:
 Reagan Miller
Project coordinator: Mark Sachner,
 Water Buffalo Books
Editors: Mark Sachner, Lynn Peppas
Proofreader: Shannon Welbourn
Indexer: Gini Holland
Editorial director: Kathy Middleton
Photo researcher: Water Buffalo Books
Designer: Westgraphix/Tammy West
**Production coordinator and prepress
 technician:** Margaret Amy Salter
Print coordinator: Katherine Berti

Written, developed, and produced by
Water Buffalo Books

Publisher's note:
All quotations in this book come from original sources and
contain the spelling and grammatical inconsistencies of
the original text. Some of the quotations may also contain
terms that are no longer in use and may be considered
inappropriate or offensive. The use of such terms is for
the sake of preserving the historical and literary accuracy
of the sources and should not be seen as encouraging or
endorsing the use of such terms today.

Photographs and reproductions:
Alamy: © Luc Novovitch: p. 4 (main); © epa european
pressphoto agency b.v.: pp. 6, 99; © JS Callahan/tropicalpix
: p. 26; © Gallo Images: p. 61 (top); © Mike Abrahams: p. 61
(bottom); © Pictorial Press Ltd: p. 76; © John Warburton-Lee
Photography: p. 79; © Africa Media Online: p. 97. Associated
Press: Dennis Lee Royle: cover (right). **Corbis:** © Paul
Almasy: p. 40; © David Turnley: p. 48; © Reuters: p. 85. **Getty
Images:** pp. 56, 63, 68, 69 (bottom), 75; Time & Life Pictures:
pp. 8, 71 (right), 86, 91 (bottom); Apic: 21; AFP: pp. 23, 84, 88,
102 (left); Popperfoto: pp. 51, 60. **Courtesy of Gini Holland:**
p. 94. **Library of Congress:** p. 101. **Public Domain:** pp.
4 (left), 5, 15 (top), 15 (bottom left), 16, 19, 29 (both), 30, 43
(top), 47, 59, 62, 64, 65, 69 (top), 71 (left), 73 (top), 73 (bottom),
81, 83, 91 (top), 92, 100. **Shutterstock:** Catwalker: pp. 12
(left), 54 (top & bottom); Popartic: p. 12 (right); 360b: p. 13;
Luke Schmidt: p. 18; Solodov Alexey: p. 43; StampGirl: p.
54 (middle); jbor: p. 102 (top right). **Wikipedia Creative
Commons:** Emi Deborah: cover (left); rodneyellis: p. 1; South
Africa The Good News: p. 4 (right); rahuldlucca: p. 10; Htonl:
p. 15 (bottom right); Lyssipos: p. 32; Mycelium101: p. 37;
Guinnog: p. 45; Samuella99: p. 53; Rob C. Croes / Anefo: p. 82;
Paul Weinberg: p. 93; Salym Fayad: p. 98.

Cover: Imprisoned for 27 years, Nelson Mandela became
a symbol in the fight against the oppression of the black
majority by South Africa's apartheid government. Following
his release from prison, he became South Africa's first
president voted into office in a truly open, democratic election.

Library and Archives Canada Cataloguing in Publication

Dakers, Diane, author
 Nelson Mandela : South Africa's anti-apartheid revolutionary /
Diane Dakers.

(Crabtree groundbreaker biographies)
Includes index.
Issued in print and electronic formats.
ISBN 978-0-7787-1241-1 (bound).--ISBN 978-0-7787-1243-5 (pbk.).--
ISBN 978-1-4271-1572-0 (pdf).--ISBN 978-1-4271-1570-6 (html)

 1. Mandela, Nelson, 1918-2013--Juvenile literature. 2. African
National Congress--Biography--Juvenile literature. 3. Anti-apartheid
movements--South Africa--Juvenile literature. 4. Political prisoners--
South Africa--Biography--Juvenile literature. 5. Civil rights workers-
-South Africa--Biography--Juvenile literature. 6. Presidents--South
Africa--Biography--Juvenile literature. 7. South Africa--Biography.
I. Title. II. Series: Crabtree groundbreaker biographies

DT1974.D35 2014   j968.06'5092   C2014-903220-X
                                       C2014-903221-8

Library of Congress Cataloging-in-Publication Data

CIP available at Library of Congress

Crabtree Publishing Company

www.crabtreebooks.com   1-800-387-7650

Printed in Canada/052014/MA20140505

**Published
in Canada**
Crabtree Publishing
616 Welland Ave.
St. Catharines, Ontario
L2M 5V6

**Published in
the United States**
Crabtree Publishing
PMB 59051
350 Fifth Ave., 59th Floor
New York, NY 10118

**Published in the
United Kingdom**
Crabtree Publishing
Maritime House
Basin Road North, Hove
BN41 1WR

**Published
in Australia**
Crabtree Publishing
3 Charles Street
Coburg North
VIC, 3058

Contents

Chapter 1
Black and White

At age 16, around the year 1934, in a traditional ritual of his Xhosa people, Nelson Mandela became a man. Before the ceremony, he and 25 other boys moved out of their tiny village at the southern tip of Africa. Away from their families for the first time, the boys lived together in grass huts on the banks of the nearby Mbashe River. There, they celebrated their last days of childhood, playing in the wild bush country, stealing a pig, and enjoying youthful camaraderie. After several weeks, they returned to the village to participate in the serious—and painful—rite of passage that would make men of them.

Boys to Men

The night before the final ceremony, the boys danced and sang with girls and women from the village, the activities becoming more and more feverish as the night passed. In the morning, they purified

Opposite: Photos of Nelson Mandela at different stages of his life. Main photo: at around the age of 72, taken in 1990 at a rally in New York City, shortly after gaining his freedom following 27 years in South African prisons. Left inset: at about the age of 19, taken around 1937. Right inset: at around the age of 90, taken in 2008.

Above: The present flag of South Africa was adopted in 1994, the year Nelson Mandela was elected to the nation's presidency. Three of the flag's colors— black, green, and yellow— are found in the banner of the African National Congress, or ANC, the nation's top party and the group to which Nelson belonged during the struggle for racial equality. Three others—red, white, and blue— are taken from flags flown when the country was under Dutch and British rule.

themselves by bathing in the cold river waters. Then the boys lined up, seated and naked, as an elderly man with an *assegai,* or spear, moved down the line. One by one, he circumcised the boys with the *assegai.* *"Ndiyindoda!"* yelled each boy after the ritual cut. "I am a man!" Immediately, each teenager was given a new name. Nelson's "circumcision name" was Dalibunga, meaning "Founder of the Bunga," the traditional ruling body of the Transkei region where he lived.

A group of Xhosa youths, wrapped in blankets, return home from the woods near their village in South Africa. They have been initiated into manhood in a ceremony similar to the one in which the young Nelson Mandela participated. The village shown here is near Qunu, where Nelson was raised and one of the places he lived following his retirement from politics in 1999.

For the next few days, the youths returned to their grass huts to heal. When they emerged, the village welcomed them home, giving them gifts, singing songs, and celebrating their newfound manhood. Village elders and important men gave speeches in their honor. The featured speaker of the day was Chief Meligqili, the son of the regional ruler. When he spoke, the ceremonial mood changed.

"There sit our sons, young, healthy and handsome, the flower of the Xhosa tribe, the pride of our nation," he said to the villagers.

"We have just circumcised them in a ritual that promises manhood, but I am here to tell you that it is an empty promise.... For we Xhosas, and all black South Africans, are a conquered people. We are slaves in our own country. We are tenants on our own soil. We have no strength, no power, no control over our own destiny in the land of our birth."

He went on, criticizing the wealthy white men who treated the black Africans as slaves, who had destroyed black African culture, and who had crushed the black Africans' spirits.

Chief Meligqili's words certainly crushed Nelson's spirits. He was angry that this man had spoiled his big day with such negative talk. He dismissed the chief's words, thinking him ignorant and ungrateful. "At the time, I looked on the white man, not as an oppressor, but as a benefactor," wrote Nelson 60 years later. This was the first time he had heard anything different, and he did not want to hear these words— not on this happy day of all days.

Before long, though, Nelson began to realize the truth of the chief's speech.

The words planted a seed that grew inside Nelson, fueling his commitment to fight for the equality of blacks in South Africa, a cause he would dedicate his life to. Those remarks "have been ringing in my ears for 40 years."

This system was called "apartheid," which means "apartness" in the Afrikaans language of the white leaders.

Darkness and Light

As Nelson grew into adulthood, he attended schools where white and non-white students did not mix. He lived in poor, crime-ridden, blacks-only communities without running water, heat, or electricity, while the wealthy white people lived lives of luxury within the same city. He was not allowed to vote in elections—only white men could vote or run for government office.

In a nation where more than 70 percent of the population was black, the white minority set the rules. Those rules were unfair at best, cruel and racist at worst. They were designed to keep white and non-white people separated. Over the years, the laws against black people became even more oppressive, or restrictive. This system was called "apartheid," which means "apartness" in the Afrikaans language of the white leaders.

BOERS AND BRITISH IN SOUTH AFRICA

For thousands of years, black tribal groups have lived in what is now South Africa. Traditionally, they were farmers and cattle herders.

In the mid 1600s, white Dutch settlers arrived, setting up a colony at what is today the city of Cape Town. These *Boers* ("farmers") gradually took over more and more territory, forcing the black Africans off their land. The Boers stole cattle and killed African men, women, and children. They brought European diseases that took the lives of even more native people. They captured blacks from other parts of Africa and kept them as slaves.

In 1806, the British arrived and took over Cape Town. They, too, fought against black Africans for control of the land. At one point, the Boers and British banded together to fight the native population, but as the British became more and more powerful, the Boers moved inland into new territories.

When gold and diamonds were discovered on Boer turf, the two white groups became rivals. After a number of battles, the British took control of the entire region. In 1910, they created the Union of South Africa as part of the British Empire. For the next 14 years, the English-speaking British ran the country, even though most of the white residents were Afrikaans-speaking Boers (also called Afrikaners).

The bitterness between the two groups of whites continued for decades. The British ran the country until 1924, when the Afrikaners won an election and took control. They declared Afrikaans (a version of Dutch) as an official language of South Africa—along with English. The Afrikaners stayed in power until Nelson Mandela became president of South Africa 70 years later.

The injustice of the government was too much for Nelson. In his early 20s, he joined the African National Congress (ANC), a group that demanded equal rights for all South Africans. With the ANC, Nelson protested, and boycotted, and spoke out in public. The more the people objected to the unfair laws, the more violent the government became in its efforts to shut them down.

Nelson was a natural leader, a well-spoken and educated young man, who quickly rose through the ranks of the ANC. He took charge, and he took risks. He eventually became one of the most wanted "traitors" in South Africa. Police arrested him over and over again. In the end, Nelson was to spend 27 years behind bars.

A "Boycott Apartheid" campaign bus on the streets of London, England, in 1989.

While he served his time in prison, the anti-apartheid fight continued in South Africa. Eventually, it spread internationally. In 1980, "Free Mandela" became a cry heard around the world. Suddenly, Nelson's 62-year-old face became the symbol of oppression. International leaders, celebrities, and everyday people demanded his release—and an end to apartheid.

White Against Black

White Europeans first moved into what is now South Africa in the 1600s. From then until the 1990s, when the nation's first truly democratic elections were won overwhelmingly by black Africans, whites did their best to crush the black African majority. First, they took land, cattle, and businesses. Then they declared war on the tribal people, killing thousands. By the time the British created the Union of South Africa in 1910, black Africans owned less than 10 percent of the country—even though they represented more than 70 percent of the population.

In 1912, in an effort to defend their rights, black Africans formed the South African Native National Congress. This organization was later renamed the African National Congress, or ANC. A year later, the white leaders responded by passing the Native Land Act. This law prohibited blacks from buying land and forced them to live on reserves.

During World War I (1914–1918), mining and other industries boomed in South Africa. Many black African men left the poor reserves to find work in the cities. They returned home a few times a year to help the women and children they'd left behind. Each black man carried a passbook at all times to prove to police he had a job and, therefore, had a right to be in the city.

In 1923, the government passed the Natives (Urban Areas) Act to control the rising black population in South Africa's cities. This law restricted the number of black people allowed to move into a city and created segregated, or separate, areas within each city for blacks to live. The goal was to keep blacks and whites apart.

When the Afrikaners took power in 1924, the situation for black South Africans continued to decline. It would be 70 years before they won equal rights in their own country.

In 1990, Nelson finally walked out of prison a free man. He was 71 years old, but his most significant work was just beginning. Nelson led his country out of apartheid, and into democracy, when he became South Africa's first black president.

Nelson Mandela's face has appeared on countless stamps, forms of currency, and magazine covers around the world. Shown here: a Mexican postage stamp honoring that country's relationship with South Africa since the fall of apartheid and a cover of Time *magazine.*

For his commitment to freedom, equal rights, and peace, Nelson was honored with hundreds of international distinctions, including the Nobel Peace Prize. Countries around the globe showered him with awards, medals, knighthoods, honorary university degrees, and citizenships. He is the subject of scores of books, films, and songs. He has been on the cover of *Time* magazine six times since 1990. His face has graced postage stamps in South Africa and around the world. He is even the subject of comic books and graphic novels.

When Nelson Mandela died in December 2013, he was given a funeral fit for royalty. It included a 10-day national mourning period and a grand memorial attended by dozens of international leaders and celebrities, and tens of thousands of local mourners. He was laid to rest in the land of his childhood, in a traditional Xhosa burial ceremony.

Flowers, candles, and images left by mourners at the South African Embassy in Berlin, Germany, as a tribute to Nelson Mandela following his death in December 2013.

As a boy, Nelson Mandela, or Rolihlahla as he was called at his birth, had lived and played in the velds, or grasslands, of South Africa. Upon his passing, almost a century later, he returned to rest in the land of his youth—but not before he had reshaped the course of history in his nation and lit a beacon of inspiration and hope to people all over the world.

Chapter 2
Rooted in Tradition

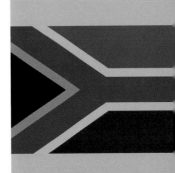

N ear the very tip of the continent of Africa, just 50 miles (80 kilometers) from the Indian Ocean, is a speck on the map, a village called Mvezo. A century ago, this tiny village, like the surrounding Transkei region of South Africa, was completely untouched by the modern world. Home to the Thembu people, members of the larger Xhosa nation, life here had barely changed in hundreds of years. It was in this tiny village, on July 18, 1918, that baby Rolihlahla Mandela—who would later be called Nelson—came into the world.

These maps show the relationship of South Africa to the rest of the world and to the continent of Africa, and the locations of the Transkei region, where Nelson Mandela was born and raised, and Johannesburg, the city where Nelson lived at various times of his life.

AFRICA

South Africa

Johannesburg

SOUTH AFRICA

Transkei

This painting, by artist Frederick Timpson I'Ons, shows a group of Xhosa people, accompanied by their dogs, resting during a hunt. Scenes like this were common up to and including the time that Nelson Mandela was born into the Xhosa nation in 1918.

Village Life

Rolihlahla's parents lived a traditional lifestyle in this land of rolling hills, green valleys, and wide-open grasslands. His father, Gadla Henry Mphakanyiswa, was chief of the village and senior advisor to the Thembu king. Like many men in Mvezo, Henry had more than one wife, and each wife had many children. Rolihlahla's mother, Nosekeni Fanny Nkedama, was the third of Henry's four wives. Rolihlahla was the eldest of Fanny's four kids, and the youngest boy of the 13 children—nine girls and four boys—fathered by Henry.

Rolihlahla's parents could neither read nor write and had never been to school. Because they were related to the royal family of the Thembu tribe, though, they were important in the village. As chief of Mvezo, Henry earned money and owned land and livestock. He was considered wealthy by local standards. Each of his wives lived in her own home, separated from the other wives and children by many miles. Henry traveled between his wives' homesteads to spend time with each of his families.

DID YOU KNOW?

In the Xhosa language, Nelson Mandela's given name, Rolihlahla, means "pulling the branch of a tree." In common usage, it also means "troublemaker."

Early in Rolihlahla's childhood, disaster struck his privileged family when his father lost his job. The story, as passed down via oral, or unwritten history, was that Henry was fired from his respected position because he defied the British government that controlled South Africa at the time. (As chief of the village, he had two bosses: the Thembu *and* the British leaders.)

It all started with a dispute over an ox. The beast's owner filed a complaint against Henry, but Henry refused to accept British law when it came to resolving the ox issue. It was a matter of principle for the proud man. He said he would only honor traditional Thembu rules in this situation. This did not sit well with the local British officials, who fired him. Henry was no longer chief of the village, and his family lost everything—money, land, and livestock.

EXTENDED FAMILY

When a man has more than one wife—as did Nelson Mandela's father—it is called polygamy (pronounced "puh-LIG-uh-mee"). Today, this practice is illegal in most parts of the world, but about 50 countries still allow it. (Nowhere in the world are women permitted to have more than one husband.) Most of the countries where polygamy is legal are in Africa, and in Middle Eastern countries dominated by the Muslim faith. It is also legal in a few Asian countries, including Indonesia, Myanmar (Burma), and Malaysia. In some nations, such as India, and Sri Lanka, polygamy is legal for Muslim men only.

In a dozen African countries—including South Africa—this type of marriage is forbidden under civil, or public law, but it is permitted under traditional, or tribal, law.

The reason polygamy is generally illegal around the world is that it is considered to be a form of human-rights abuse against women. In 2000, the United Nations said polygamy promotes marriage inequality and "violates the dignity of women."

HISTORY LESSONS

Before written language existed, people used storytelling, songs, and poetry to preserve their culture. Using these oral, or vocal, methods, parents would pass down the history of their families and communities to their children, who would, in turn, pass the information to their children. Through this "oral tradition," cultural histories have survived for many generations.

The development of written language is very new for many indigenous, or aboriginal (native), cultures around the world. In fact, some people still rely on folktales, chants, and even dances to preserve the past.

Some people say oral histories are not as accurate as written histories because they rely on the memory of the person telling the story or singing the song. On the other hand, written records may be equally unreliable, because they are told from the viewpoint of the writer, and may leave out the "other side of the story." Two versions of the same story—such as the story of how Nelson Mandela's father lost his job—might be dramatically different. Who's to say which version is correct?

Suddenly baby Rolihlahla and his parents were poor. The boy and his mother moved to a nearby village called Qunu to live with his mom's relatives. His father visited for one week a month.

A second version of this story came to light a few years ago. This one is based on recently discovered, very detailed documents kept by

These round mud huts with thatched roofs are similar to the kind Nelson Mandela lived in as a boy.

SPARKLING SOIL

In 1868, prospectors discovered diamonds in South Africa. In 1886, they also found gold. Suddenly, land that had appeared dry, barren, and worthless was incredibly valuable. White Europeans flooded into the country, hoping to stake a claim to the riches. They built towns, roads, and railways. They established trading relationships with the United States and European countries. South Africa quickly became the largest diamond- and gold-producing region in the world.

As the mines grew, the mining companies gradually took control of traditional tribal land—and the black Africans who lived there. Forced off their small farms, the Africans turned to the mines to make a living. While the white mine owners raked in the riches, the black workers earned poverty-level wages.

By 1900, most of South Africa was owned by European whites. Today, South Africa remains one of the world's richest sources of diamonds and gold.

This photograph, taken at a large diamond mine in Kimberley, South Africa, in 1873, shows a group of African workers. Their white overseers, in white shirts, are shown at left. Like the men shown here, an estimated 50,000 workers used picks and shovels to dig the massive hole created at this mine between 1871 and 1918.

the regional government of the day. According to this telling of the tale, Henry wasn't simply involved in a one-time clash with the law—he had a long history of corruption, dishonesty, and abuse of power within the village. Eventually, he stood trial, and a number of villagers testified against him. The British judge found Henry guilty and dismissed him from his post. These newfound documents show that Rolihlahla was eight years old when his father was fired, and his mother and her children had already been living in Qunu for several years by this time.

No matter when he moved there, Rolihlahla loved living in this new, larger village. He still enjoyed a traditional lifestyle, playing with his cousins in the grasslands, sleeping in a round mud hut, and listening to stories about great Xhosa warriors. He also worked hard, planting and harvesting crops, tending goats, and milking cows alongside his mother and younger sisters.

During her time in Qunu, Rolihlahla's mother became a devout Christian, even though her husband remained devoted to the great spirit of the Xhosas. While he continued to practice traditional Xhosa rituals, she attended church. When the missionaries who ran the church suggested she send her son to school, she listened. Thus, at age seven, the same year he was baptized in the Methodist religion, Rolihlahla became the first in his family ever to attend school.

Nelson Goes to School

Until now, Rolihlahla had always worn the traditional Xhosa clothing for boys, a blanket wrapped around one shoulder and pinned at the waist. When it came time to start school, though, Henry insisted his son dress properly for classes. Rolihlahla was to wear pants for the first time:

"My father took a pair of his trousers and cut them at the knee. They were roughly the correct length, although the waist was far too large. My father took a piece of string and cinched the trousers at the waist. I must have been a comical sight, but I have never owned a suit I was prouder to wear than my father's cut-off pants."

Nelson Mandela as a young man, wearing clothing that is similar to what he wore as a young boy before he started attending British missionary school.

On the first day of school, Rolihlahla happily marched into the one-room schoolhouse with the other children. His teacher was a British missionary whose goal was to provide local people with an education that included bringing them closer to Christianity. That day, Rolihlahla's teacher gave each African child an English name. On that day, Rolihlahla became Nelson.

"Africans of my generation—and even today—generally have both an English and an African name," said Nelson. "Whites were either unable or unwilling to pronounce an African name, and considered it uncivilized to have one."

That day, Rolihlahla's teacher gave each African child an English name. On that day, Rolihlahla became Nelson.

Five years later, when Nelson was 12, his father Henry died unexpectedly, leaving his four wives with no support. Wisely, though, just before his death, Henry had arranged for the grand leader of all Thembu people to look after his youngest son. Chief Jongintaba Dalindyebo, who was related to Henry, agreed to become Nelson's guardian and mentor.

After a short period of mourning for his father, Nelson and his mother walked the 6 miles (10 km) from Qunu to Mqhekezweni, where the grand chief lived. A few days later, his mom turned around and walked home, leaving her son at "The Great Place," as the chief's palace was called. "Even as my mother and first friend was leaving, my head was swimming with the delights of my new home," wrote Nelson many years later. "To me it was a magical kingdom; everything was delightful."

In this photo, the grounds of "The Great Place" are shown as they look today. This is where Nelson moved when he was 12, following the death of his father. The tree is one of several under which local meetings were held by Nelson's guardian and mentor, Chief Jongintaba Dalindyebo.

The palace was the largest, grandest home Nelson had ever seen. Surrounding it were a number of other beautiful, gleaming white buildings, a church, orchards, fields, and gardens. Grazing outside this central area were horses, along with dozens of cattle and hundreds of sheep. Chief Jongintaba also owned a huge shiny car! Everyone wore expensive, Western-style clothing. Nelson had never experienced such luxury.

At his new school, a one-room schoolhouse next to the palace, Nelson studied English, Xhosa, history, and geography with the other children who lived at "The Great Place". They were all related to one another, and they soon became his new sisters and brothers. Nelson particularly admired Jongintaba's eldest son Justice, who was in high school when they met. "He was four years older than I and became my first hero after my father."

When he wasn't at school, Nelson had chores to do. He helped plow the fields, care for the animals, and iron the chief's suits. He also had plenty of playtime with the other boys, riding horses, shooting at birds with slingshots, and having make-believe sword fights.

Nelson thrived at "The Great Place". He worked hard at school and learned leadership skills by observing Jongintaba's ways. He paid close attention to the chief's problem-solving skills. Somehow, Jongintaba always managed to settle disputes among the Thembu people in a way that respected the interests of everyone involved. This was a leadership lesson that Nelson would take into adulthood.

The Boy Becomes a Man

When he was 16, Nelson left his boyhood behind when he took part in the traditional Thembu coming-of-age ritual. Along with 25 other boys, including Justice, he spent two months living in grass huts in the isolated bushland along the banks of the Mbashe River. "It was a sacred time," said Nelson. "I felt happy and fulfilled taking part in my people's customs."

One of those customs decreed that the boys "perform a daring exploit" before their final transition from boyhood to manhood. "In days of old, this might have involved a cattle raid or even a battle," said Nelson. "But in our time, the deeds were more mischievous than martial." Rather than going to war, he and his friends stole a pig, killed it, built a fire, and ate a roast pork dinner under the stars.

The final—and most sacred—part of the rite of passage was the circumcision ceremony. While drums pounded, and friends and relatives watched from a distance, the boys lined up, seated on a blanket, their legs stretched out in front of them. An elderly *ingcibi*, or traditional surgeon, moved down the line, stopping briefly in front of each boy. With his *assegai*, or spear, he quickly cut the foreskin of each boy's penis. To show their bravery, the boys were not to flinch or cry, despite the great pain of the operation. "A boy may cry; a man conceals his pain," said Nelson.

Nelson believed the whites were good people who had brought education and benefits to South Africa.

After this excruciating procedure, which in most cultures is performed within days of an infant boy's birth, the young men painted their bodies with white clay and returned to their huts to heal. Several days later, they emerged and bathed in the river, to wash away the white

A group of present-day Xhosa boys cover their bodies with white clay as part of their rite of passage from boyhood into manhood. The ritual they are observing is the same as that practiced by boys and young men in Xhosa culture for centuries.

coating on their bodies. Then they repainted themselves, this time with red ocher, a natural pigment from the earth. After another ritual bathing, the young men burned down their grass huts to symbolize their leaving behind all remnants of childhood, once and for all.

They returned to the village, where their friends and families celebrated their transition from boyhood to manhood. It was during this ceremony that the respected Chief Maligqili made the speech Nelson would never forget. He said these young men would never reach their potential as future leaders, scholars, or soldiers because the white men who ruled South Africa would hold them back. Said the chief:

"The abilities, the intelligence, the promise of these young men will be squandered in their attempt to eke out a living doing the simplest, most mindless chores for the white man. These gifts today are [nothing], for we cannot give them the greatest gift of all, which is freedom and independence."

Nelson was angry that Chief Meligqili had dampened the happy spirit of the day by speaking ill of the white men. He believed the whites were good people who had brought education and benefits to South Africa. How dare this chief, this "ignorant man," utter such "abusive comments," he thought to himself. "I thought the chief was enormously ungrateful. [He] was ruining my day, spoiling the proud feeling with wrong-headed remarks."

It would not be long, though, before Nelson began to see the truth in the chief's words.

Chapter 3
Living and Learning in a White Man's World

Because his father had been a village chief, and because he had royal blood in his veins, Nelson Mandela was destined to become a leader in his community. In fact, Chief Jongintaba was already grooming him to become an advisor to the next Thembu king. That meant Nelson needed a proper education at a well-respected school.

Higher Education

In 1934, shortly after the manhood ceremony, the chief sent 16-year-old Nelson to live and study at Clarkebury Boarding School, about 40 miles (65 km) away. Clarkebury was the most advanced school in the region, and Nelson excelled in his studies—not because he was smarter than the other students, but because he worked hard and he had a good memory. He graduated in two years, instead of the usual three.

From there, he moved on to Healdtown, a much larger, even more impressive British-style boarding school. The chief's son, Justice, was already a student there. Located about

Chief Jongintaba Dalindyebo, the Thembu grand leader and relative of Nelson Mandela's father, Henry. Under his guidance, Nelson became a part of a larger family and developed leadership skills that shaped not only his youth but his future as a public figure. He also developed an independent spirit that would become a challenge to Jongintaba as Nelson's guardian!

185 miles (300 km) from "The Great Place", as the chief's palace was called, Healdtown was home to more than 1,000 students—men and women, members of different African tribes, blacks and whites. Despite this diverse population, the different ethnic groups did not socialize together. Still, through his classes, Nelson met members of many different tribes. He met new friends, including his first-ever non-Xhosa friend, and his first-ever female friend. He even got to know an African teacher who married a woman from a different tribe— something Nelson had believed was forbidden. For the first time, said Nelson, "I began to sense my identity as an African, not just a Thembu or even a Xhosa."

At Healdtown, Nelson enjoyed a number of new experiences. He had his first taste of leadership when he became a prefect, or student-in-charge, at his dormitory. He took up long-distance running, an activity that allowed him "to escape from the hurly-burly of school life." He also discovered boxing, a sport that was to become a lifelong passion.

During Nelson's second and final year at Healdtown, he was excited to attend a talk by a famous Xhosa poet named Mqhayi. The poet was so well respected that the day he visited Healdtown was declared a school holiday.

Nelson Mandela in 1937, around the time when he was a student at Healdtown.

Like Chief Meligqili, who had made the speech that shocked Nelson at the circumcision ceremony, Mqhayi talked about the dangers of allowing African culture to be crushed by white outsiders. "We cannot allow these foreigners who do not care for our culture to take over our nation," said Mqhayi in his address to the students. "For too long, we have succumbed to the false gods of the white man. But we will emerge and cast off these foreign notions."

At the end of the speech, the audience, including Nelson, jumped up and applauded. In that moment, Nelson was proud to be a Xhosa man, and proud to be African, but confused over his place in his own country. He began to question why the white minority held power over the black majority in South Africa. He wondered about his future, what kind of person he would become as an African man educated in a white school system. Like other privileged African students at Healdtown, Nelson had sometimes been called a "Black Englishman," a term that had, up until now, fit with his goals. Suddenly, he wasn't sure if that was who he wanted to be.

A few months later, after graduating from Healdtown, Nelson, now 20, began working toward a Bachelor of Arts degree at the nearby University of Fort Hare. There he studied English, politics, Dutch law, and native administration. This course of study was designed to prepare him for a career as a translator in the government—the best job a black man could hope for at the time. Outside class hours, Nelson continued cross-country running and boxing, but he also took up soccer,

LEADERSHIP SCHOOL

In 1939, Nelson Mandela began his studies at the University of Fort Hare. Founded by missionaries in 1916 as the South African Native College, the school became the leading college for black students in southern Africa. Nelson may have been the most famous student to study there, but he certainly wasn't the only leader to attend classes at Fort Hare.

Future presidents of Botswana, Tanzania, Zimbabwe, and Zambia studied there, as did many up-and-coming lawyers, politicians, writers, and filmmakers. Famous peace activist Archbishop Desmond Tutu became the university's chaplain, or religious leader, in 1967.

In 1959, Fort Hare became a segregated school for Xhosa students only. The quality of instruction declined over the years. Outspoken staff members and students were expelled. Finally, in 1990, when all South Africans—black and white—were declared equal under the law, Fort Hare once again became open to everyone.

An old building at the University of Fort Hare, where Nelson attended college. As its name would suggest, Fort Hare was originally a military outpost—a British fort during wars between the Xhosa and British settlers in the 1800s.

drama, bible studies, and ballroom dancing. On the soccer field, he met a science student named Oliver Tambo, who would become his lifelong friend and business partner.

A small, elite school with fewer than 200 students, Fort Hare was even more culturally diverse than Nelson's previous schools had been. Before long, he had friends from every political and ethnic background. He was popular, charismatic and athletic. In his second year, Nelson was elected, along with five others, to the student council. Only 25 students voted in the election. The rest boycotted the vote to protest the living conditions, particularly the poor food, at the college. They also believed the student government should have a stronger voice within the school system. The six elected student representatives quit immediately after the elections, to support the student protest.

A few days later, the school held a repeat election. The only students who voted this time were the same 25 who had voted the first time. Again, Nelson was elected to the student council, and again, he refused to serve because

DOUBLE TROUBLE

Nelson and his "brother" Justice got into such mischief together that, when they were reunited at "The Great Place", Chief Jongintaba did his best to keep them separated. It didn't work. The young men soon proved the chief was right to worry about their trouble-making tendencies when they ran away to Johannesburg. To earn money to buy train tickets, Nelson and Justice stole two of Chief Jongintaba's prize cows. They sold the animals and paid someone to drive them to the train station, where they bought two tickets to the big city.

PERFECT STRANGER

In some cultures, young men and women don't necessarily marry for love. They marry because their parents tell them to, and they marry the people they are told to marry. This tradition is called arranged marriage, and until the 1700s, it was common practice around the world. Today, it is still practiced in some parts of Asia, Africa, the Middle East, and Latin America.

In a typical arranged marriage, a young person's parents or grandparents choose a suitable spouse. In some cultures, it is a matchmaker or priest who makes the selection. The choice may be influenced by family values, reputation, religion, wealth, career goals, appearance, or even medical history.

In most cases today, the future bride or groom has some say in the process. If they reject the parents' first choice, mom and dad will find someone else. In some cases, though, a bride might not even meet her future husband until her wedding day. There are also still cultures in which marriages are arranged while the future bride and groom are still children.

he believed the school's governing system was flawed. This time, though, the other five students who had been elected agreed to serve as student representatives.

The principal called Nelson to his office and told him he was suspended from school until he agreed to take his elected position. Nelson refused, so the principal sent him home to Chief Jongintaba, who was furious over Nelson's actions.

Back at "The Great Place", Nelson was delighted to be reunited with Justice, who had returned to Mqhekezweni after graduating from Healdtown. But the young men's happy reunion was short-lived. If they were not going to continue their education, said Chief Jongintaba, they were to remain in the village and marry women he had chosen for them. The idea of arranged marriages didn't sit well with Nelson or Justice. Rather than marry women they didn't love, they ran away to the big city of Johannesburg, about 560 miles (900 km) away. Their plan was to find work in the gold mines.

Life in the Big City

Nelson and Justice easily found jobs in Johannesburg. Because he was the son of a tribal chief, Justice landed the most desirable position, as a clerk in a mining office. Nelson got a less prestigious job working as night watchman for the same mining company. After just a few days, though, a furious Chief Jongintaba sent word to the mine manager that Nelson and Justice did not have his permission to be in Johannesburg. "Send boys home at once," he demanded in a telegram. Instead of going home, though, the boys split up, each finding a place to live, so they could stay in the city.

Nelson, now 22 years old, moved in with his cousin, Garlick Mbekeni, a clothing salesman who lived in Johannesburg. Garlick was well connected and knew some influential people. When Nelson announced that his dream was to become a lawyer, Garlick introduced him to Walter Sisulu, "one of our best people in Johannesburg."

Walter was a real estate agent and political activist six years older than Nelson. Because most blacks in South Africa were not allowed to own property—meaning they didn't need an estate agent—Walter's role in his community was closer to that of a social worker.

He liked Nelson immediately. "When he came into my office, I marked him at once as a man with great qualities, who was destined to play an important part," Walter said about Nelson. Walter helped Nelson get a job as a clerk and messenger at a local law firm.

In Alexandra, Nelson saw, firsthand, the poverty and racism blacks lived with, while the rich whites thrived in the city.

By day, Nelson worked at the law offices of Witkin, Sidelsky and Eidelman, a rare group of white lawyers who handled cases for both white and black clients. These lawyers were also open-minded enough to hire a black clerk, something that was simply not done in Johannesburg at the time. Blacks and whites did not mix, and they certainly did not work together.

At night, Nelson continued his studies by correspondence, working toward finishing the university degree he'd begun at Fort Hare. He rented a room in a small house in Alexandra, a poor, black, crime-ridden part of Johannesburg. His new home was "a tin-roofed room at the back of the property, no more than a shack, with a dirt floor, no heat, no electricity, no running water," he said. "But it was a place of my own, and I was happy to have it."

In Alexandra, Nelson saw, firsthand, the poverty and racism blacks lived with, while the rich whites thrived in the city. Also called "the Dark City" because it had no electricity, and therefore no lights, Alexandra was dirty, noisy, and overcrowded. It was home to gangsters, armed hoodlums, and illegal drinking parlors. Wrote Nelson:

"It could fairly be described as a slum. The roads were unpaved and dirty, and filled with hungry, undernourished children scampering around half-naked. The air was thick with smoke from coal fires in tin stoves. A single water tap served several houses."

Like most of his neighbors in Alexandra, Nelson lived in poverty. He often went hungry and never had new clothes. For years, he wore the same suit every day, one that his boss, Mr. Sidelsky, had given him. Nelson said he mended that suit so often that, eventually, "there were more patches than suit." Sometimes, to save on bus fare, he walked the six miles (nine km) from Alexandra to his workplace.

Residents gather in front of a collection of woven art in this scene from the Alexandra township in Johannesburg, South Africa. Although it has undergone many changes since the days when Nelson Mandela lived there in the 1940s, Alexandra remains one of the poorest urban areas in the nation.

THE BABY WHO WOULD BE KING

The Thembu people are led by a king, or "paramount chief." When one king dies, the eldest son of his first wife (he may have many wives) becomes the next king. And so on. At least, this is how it usually goes. In the early 20th century, this pattern was broken when the reigning king died very young. His eldest son, Sabata, was still a baby at the time, so clearly he was not able to rule his people. In this case, the deceased king's next-eldest brother became the paramount chief.

That man was Jongintaba, who later became Nelson Mandela's guardian. Because he wasn't born to be the grand ruler, Chief Jongintaba was sort of an acting king until Sabata grew up. When Jongintaba died in 1942, Sabata was only 13 years old—still too young to take his position as paramount chief of the Thembu people. Instead, another of Jongintaba's brothers stepped into the role.

Sabata finally became king, or paramount chief, in 1954, when he was 25 years old.

At night, he studied by candlelight because he couldn't afford an oil lamp.

All Nelson's hard work and sacrifice paid off, though, when he finally earned his Bachelor of Arts degree at age 24. Early in 1943, he proudly returned to Fort Hare to attend his graduation ceremony. A few months later, he took another step toward realizing his dream of becoming a lawyer when he enrolled part-time at the University of the Witwatersrand. He was the only black law student.

New Friends

A few months after Nelson and Justice ran off to Johannesburg, Chief Jongintaba paid them a visit. When he met with Nelson, he asked the young man about his plans for the future, his work, and his studies. "He recognized that my life was starting to … take a different course from the one he had envisaged and planned," said Nelson.

The chief did not try to change Nelson's plans, even though he had been grooming Nelson for a different life. He didn't try to convince Nelson to return to Mqhekezweni. He accepted Nelson's new career goals. After all, Nelson was now a grown man, no longer in the care of his father's royal relative. At the same time, though, the visit with the chief reminded Nelson how much he loved his homeland, its people, and the Thembu traditions, things he had forgotten about in the early excitement of his new life in the big city.

Justice didn't get off so easily when he met with his father. Because he was destined to become chief when Jongintaba died, tradition decreed that Justice must return to "The Great Place" immediately. Justice refused, even when Nelson tried to convince him to go home.

It was only when Jongintaba died less than a year later, in August 1942, that Justice returned to Mqhekezweni. He and Nelson traveled there together when they heard the sad news. Nelson stayed in the village for a week before returning to Johannesburg. Justice stayed behind to be with his family, but eventually returned to the city.

Meanwhile, through his work at the law firm, Nelson had begun to make new friends in Johannesburg. Through these friends, he started to be drawn into the world of politics.

An apartheid-era bus stop in Johannesburg with *"EUROPEANS ONLY"* painted on it in English and Afrikaans. Before the dismantling of the apartheid system in the 1990s, most black Africans were not allowed to live in central Johannesburg. Those who worked in Johannesburg were forced to commute to and from their homes outside of the city. In 1943, when the bus company raised its fares by 25 percent, thousands of commuters boycotted the buses. The bus company, feeling the heat of the boycott, lost money and returned its fares to their previous rate.

One of his new friends, a black African co-worker named Gaur Redebe, was particularly active in fighting racism and trying to improve the lives of blacks. He took Nelson to political meetings, loaned him books, and educated him on the history of oppression in Africa. He also helped organize the first mass protest Nelson ever attended. It was a nine-day boycott of the local bus system.

The "Native Bus" provided black-only transportation for Africans from Alexandra to downtown Johannesburg, where many of the passengers worked. In 1943, the bus company raised the fare by 25 percent, angering the passengers. For more than a week, about 10,000 commuters—including Nelson—boycotted the buses. They walked great distances to work, blocking roads and traffic, to protest the increased bus fare. During this time, the bus company lost money because the buses ran empty. Eventually, the bus owners gave in and returned to the lower rate.

For Nelson, the boycott was eye opening. "I found that to march with one's people was exhilarating and inspiring," he said. "But I was also impressed with the boycott's effectiveness." He had witnessed, for the first time of many to come, the power of a group of people united in a cause.

From this moment on, Nelson was no longer merely an observer of the racism, unfair rules, and cruelty his people experienced in their own country. He was now an active participant in the struggle to free black Africans from white dominance.

Chapter 4
ANC and Activism

In 1942, a year before the bus boycott, Nelson Mandela's friend Walter Sisulu had encouraged him to join the African National Congress, or ANC. The goals of this political organization, founded in 1912, were to unite black Africans, improve their living conditions, and fight racism. As soon as Nelson started attending ANC meetings, he knew this was where he belonged. This was where he was needed. He also realized that, because of his British-style education and privileged upbringing, he was on the verge of becoming just the kind of person the ANC scorned— an "elite" black man who lived by the white man's rules. He knew he could no longer be that person.

No More "Black Englishman"

Over the next two years, Nelson became more and more active within the ANC. It seemed to him and others, though, that the ANC had lost its fighting spirit. With that in mind, he and Walter and a few colleagues co-founded the ANC Youth League in 1944. Led by a passionate activist named Anton Lembede, this group took a more youthful, radical, and inclusive approach to fighting the injustices faced by black Africans. Nelson's friend from Fort Hare, Oliver

Below: A postage stamp honoring the 70th anniversary of the African National Congress (ANC), issued in the 1980s by the former Soviet Union (made up of modern Russia, Ukraine, and other states that are now independent republics).

Tambo, was the League's first secretary, Walter served as treasurer, and Nelson helped write the organization's manifesto.

FROM THE ANC YOUTH LEAGUE MANIFESTO:

- We believe that the national liberation of Africans will be achieved by Africans themselves. We reject foreign leadership of Africa.

- We believe in the unity of all Africans from the Mediterranean Sea in the North to the Indian and Atlantic oceans in the South—and that Africans must speak with one voice.

Around the same time, other non-white groups were also becoming more active in their opposition to white rule in South Africa. In 1946, the African Mine Worker's Union staged a massive strike, demanding increased wages and better working conditions. About 60,000 people participated in the protest, which lasted four days. The government reacted to the workers' job action by sending in police, who brutally attacked the protesters. They battered some workers with clubs and opened fire on others. By the end of the strike, nine workers were dead and more than 1,200 had been injured. Dozens of others were in jail. "In the end, the state prevailed," wrote Nelson. "The strike was suppressed and the union crushed."

Despite the tragic outcome, the mineworkers' protest demonstrated to Nelson once again that there was strength in numbers. When people came together, united in a single cause, they could make a difference.

INSPIRING NELSON: ANTON LEMBEDE

The oldest of seven children born to a poor farm worker and teacher, Anton Lembede was born in January 1914. He grew up in a village about 250 miles (400 km) northeast of Qunu, where Nelson Mandela was raised. Anton's mother homeschooled her son until the fourth grade. At 13, Anton began his formal education, eventually becoming a teacher and a lawyer.

Anton was a brilliant young man who fought for freedom and equality for black Africans. He was the brains behind the ANC Youth League, which he co-founded with Nelson, Walter Sisulu, and others. Anton was the organization's first president. He died suddenly of heart failure in 1947. He was only 33 years old.

This view was reinforced later that year when South Africa's Indian population began what would become a two-year "passive resistance campaign." About three percent of South Africa's population is made up of people who migrated, or whose ancestors migrated, from India. In addition to people of mixed race, South African law discriminated against Indians and

An apartheid-era sign restricting a beach in Durban, South Africa, to "the sole use of members of the white race group." Durban, one of South Africa's biggest cities, is home to the nation's largest population of people of Indian descent. During the time of apartheid, Indians suffered most of the same discrimination as blacks and people of mixed race.

other Asians. At the time, the government classified as "colored" people of mixed race as well as Indians and anyone else who wasn't black or white. In 1946, thousands of Indians from all walks of life held rallies, picketed white-owned land, and disobeyed racist rules. More than 2,000 people voluntarily went to jail for breaking laws that had been designed to exclude Indians from "whites-only" areas and activities. Said Nelson of the Indians' campaign:

"The Indian campaign became a model for the type of protest that we in the Youth League were calling for. It instilled a spirit of defiance and radicalism among the people, broke the fear of prison, and boosted the popularity of the [Indian organizations]."

It also, along with the mineworkers' strike, raised awareness within South Africa of the nation's racist regime, or system of government.

"Apartheid was a new term but an old idea," said Nelson.

First Family

In 1944, Nelson Mandela met and married a student nurse named Evelyn Mase. "I think I loved him the first time I saw him," said Evelyn, who was 23 at the time. The couple could not afford a proper wedding celebration, so they got married at the Native Commissioner's Court—like getting married at city hall today.

At first, the Mandelas lived with Evelyn's relatives, but they soon moved into a home of their own in a district called Orlando. That was where "the better class of native" lived, said Nelson.

They had four children, two boys and two girls. The couple's eldest son, Madiba Thembekile ("Thembi") was born in February 1946. He died in a car crash in 1969, at age 23. The second son, Makgatho Lewanika, born in 1950, became a lawyer. He died of AIDS in 2005. The first girl, Makaziwe, who was born in 1947, died at age nine months. When the second daughter came along in 1953, Nelson and Evelyn gave her the same name, to honor their first daughter. Today, Makaziwe is a businesswoman in South Africa. She was at her father's side when he died in December 2013.

For the most part, Nelson and Evelyn lived separate lives. She was not particularly interested in politics, something that took up most of his time. They divorced in 1958.

Apartheid

In 1948, after a whites-only general election, the National Party took power in South Africa. Black Africans and Indians had not been allowed to cast ballots—and the National Party had campaigned with slogans that promised (in nastier words) that they would keep blacks in their place and kick the "coloreds" out of the country. At that time, whites made up only

Under apartheid, all black African men (and later women as well) were forced to carry passbooks that allowed them access to white areas only for special purposes, such as going to work. Serving as internal "passports" that identified blacks as to their tribal affiliation, rather than as full-fledged citizens of South Africa, they were part of the system that denied blacks the right to vote in South African elections.

about 15 percent of the population, compared to a black population of about 75 percent.

The new prime minister's first move after his election was to establish apartheid laws. "Apartheid was a new term but an old idea," said Nelson. The word means "apartness," and that was the goal of the new government policy. Suddenly, unofficial rules that had been in place to separate whites and non-whites, and to restrict the rights of non-whites, became laws, and violations became punishable offenses.

People were to be classified by race—white, Bantu (black), and colored. Each race was to live in its own area, with separate education, transportation, and health care systems. "Whites-only" libraries, movie theaters, beaches, even park benches sprang up around the country. Black men had to carry passes to prove they had permission to enter white areas. Said Nelson:

"From the moment of the nationalists' election, we knew that our land would henceforth be a place of tension and strife."

As the black African population grew more displeased with white authority, the ANC Youth League, with its more aggressive methods, became more influential within the mainstream ANC. In the late 1940s, Youth League leaders, including Walter Sisulu, Oliver Tambo, and Nelson Mandela, were elected to executive positions within the ANC. Under their leadership, the ANC officially adopted the Youth League's goals—freedom, justice, and equal rights for all citizens. The organization also adopted the Youth League's less polite methods of achieving these goals.

Under its new "Programme of Action," the ANC stepped up its protest activities. Boycotts, rallies, civil disobedience, and strikes became more common. Throughout all its actions, though, the ANC maintained a policy of nonviolence, even when the government responded with brutality.

The ANC considered the campaign a success because it showed the government that people were prepared to rise up against injustice.

On May 1, 1950, a number of organizations banded together to stage a national day of protest against the government's racist policies. They called it Freedom Day. To try to maintain control, the government banned any meetings

Song of Peace

On June 26, 1952, when Nelson was arrested in Johannesburg, he and the other prisoners sang as they entered their jail cells. They chanted "Nkosi Sikelel' iAfrika," or "God bless Africa." This Xhosa hymn was written in 1897, and it became the national anthem of South Africa in 1994. That night in Johannesburg, it made for a "hauntingly beautiful" moment, said Nelson.

or gatherings on that day, but that didn't stop the people. More than two-thirds of African workers stayed home from work on May 1, and about 10,000 people rallied in Johannesburg. That same evening, as Nelson and Walter watched, a group of police officers on horseback rode into an orderly crowd of protesters. "All of a sudden, they started firing in our direction," remembered Nelson:

"We dove to the ground, and remained there as mounted police galloped into the crowd, smashing people with batons. We took refuge in a nearby nurses' dormitory, where we heard bullets smashing into the wall of the building."

Eighteen unarmed citizens died at police hands that night.

Over the next few years, every time the ANC and other non-white groups took action, the government responded by creating even more repressive laws. With each new law designed to keep blacks down, the ANC grew in power and in membership numbers. The organization increased its activities and continued to band together with other protest groups.

Together, they launched the Defiance Campaign Against Unjust Laws in 1952. Nelson was one of the organizers of this activity. The campaign began on June 26, 1952, when 33 volunteers walked through the "whites-only" entrance to a train station in Port Elizabeth. This was illegal, and the volunteers expected to be arrested. They were. That same day, 52 other volunteers were arrested in Johannesburg, for defying "whites-only" rules. Nelson spent the day at a demonstration in a nearby city. That night, he was arrested, along with about 50 others, for attending another meeting in Johannesburg. This was the first

Members of a crowd of black African protesters raise their voices and carry signs at a rally in Johannesburg, in 1952, in defiance of a government ban on such gatherings.

of many times he would be arrested. After two days in jail, Nelson was released on bail. Ultimately, the judge gave him a suspended sentence, meaning he didn't serve any more jail time.

The Defiance Campaign Against Unjust Laws lasted six months. By the time it ended, more than 8,000 people had been arrested without committing a single act of violence. The government's response to the campaign

SOPHIATOWN

Originally built as a white neighborhood, Sophiatown ended up as one of the few suburbs of Johannesburg where black Africans could own property. That's because it was near a sewage plant where white people didn't want to live. By the 1940s, Sophiatown was home to almost 60,000 mostly black people. It was a dirty, overcrowded, crime-ridden slum area, but it was also a center of lively black culture. Writers, musicians, and artists lived there.

In the late 1940s, white residents in nearby suburbs wanted to get rid of the black people living next door. In 1950, the government established new laws to further separate whites and non-whites. That meant police could legally force blacks to leave Sophiatown—after all, it was supposed to be a white area, and it bordered on other white areas.

Beginning in 1953, residents staged regular protests in Sophiatown to oppose the forced removal. Nelson Mandela took a lead role in this campaign. At one of the demonstrations, he admitted publically for the first time that nonviolence was "a useless strategy" in the fight for equal rights. "I said violence was the only weapon that would destroy apartheid, and we must be prepared, in the future, to use that weapon."

In the end, the Sophiatown protests had no impact. In February 1955, armed police forcibly removed thousands of residents and trucked them to their new homes.

For Nelson, Sophiatown was a turning point. "At a certain point," he said, "one can only fight fire with fire."

was to establish even stricter laws. Still, the ANC considered the campaign a success because it showed the government that people were prepared to rise up against injustice, and they weren't afraid of going to jail for standing up for what they believed in. ANC membership numbers exploded from 20,000 to 100,000 during the campaign, and Nelson had emerged as one of the ANC's leaders.

On the other hand, the government used the campaign to "prove" to whites that blacks and Indians were dangerous, that they couldn't be trusted.

The Rise of Nelson Mandela

In 1947, Nelson left his job at the law firm of Witkin, Sidelsky and Eidelman to focus on his law studies full time at the University of the Witwatersrand. This put great financial strain on him and his young wife. In addition, because

The Great Hall of the University of the Witwatersrand, where Nelson Mandela studied law. Although he was the only black African student in Witwatersrand's law school and left the school before earning his degree, he associated with students of many other backgrounds, including liberal and communist Indians, Jews, and Europeans.

of his increasing political activities, Nelson had little time for schoolwork. He failed his final exams several times and ultimately quit school without earning his law degree.

In South Africa at the time, though, there was another way for Nelson to become a lawyer—by taking a single qualifying exam. He studied hard, passed this exam, and in the midst of the Defiance Campaign, in August 1952, he set up his own law practice.

Meanwhile, Nelson's friend and former schoolmate, Oliver Tambo, had also become a lawyer in Johannesburg. Late in 1952, the two young men joined together and established their own company, Mandela and Tambo, the first black law firm in South Africa. Together, Nelson and Oliver provided legal services for ordinary Africans who found themselves on the wrong side of confusing apartheid laws.

Under those same laws, the offices of Mandela and Tambo were actually illegal—but the two young lawyers refused to stop. They constantly struggled against white judges and witnesses who refused to acknowledge their questions in the courtrooms. At one point, the law society tried to force Nelson and Oliver to stop practicing, but miraculously, the Supreme Court allowed them to continue.

Around the same time that Nelson and Oliver opened their law firm, Nelson became president of the Youth League and a regional president of the ANC. The government began monitoring his every movement and restricting his activities. In December 1952, the government imposed its first banning order on the young leader. For six months, Nelson was forbidden to leave Johannesburg, and forbidden to attend a meeting or gathering of any sort—he couldn't even attend a birthday party for his son!

EXCERPT FROM THE FREEDOM CHARTER

"We, the People of South Africa, declare for all our country and the world to know:
     that South Africa belongs to all who live in it, black and white, and that no government can justly claim authority unless it is based on the will of all the people;
     that our people have been robbed of their birthright to land, liberty and peace by a form of government founded on injustice and inequality;
     that our country will never be prosperous or free until all our people live in brotherhood, enjoying equal rights and opportunities....
     And therefore, we, the people of South Africa, black and white together—equals, countrymen and brothers—adopt this Freedom Charter;
     And we pledge ourselves to strive together, sparing neither strength nor courage, until the democratic changes here set out have been won."

Nelson Mandela stands beside his desk at the law firm he started with his friend and former schoolmate, Oliver Tambo, in 1952. The name of their firm—"MANDELA & TAMBO Attorneys"— is visible on the frosted window behind Nelson.

Over the next decade, Nelson was subjected to ban after ban after ban. Police followed him everywhere he went to make sure he abided by the rules—but he still managed to hold secret meetings to help plan protests and events. In 1955, he and other banned leaders organized the Freedom Charter Campaign. They sent thousands of volunteers all over South Africa to ask people what was important to them, what they wanted changed. They compiled the results into one final document. "The Freedom Charter is a mixture of practical goals and poetic language," said Nelson. In addition to calling for an end to racism and demanding equal rights for all South Africans, "it captures the hopes and dreams of the people, and acted as a blueprint for the liberation struggle and the future of the nation."

On June 25 and 26, 1955, Nelson and Walter Sisulu (who was also under a banning order) watched from the sidelines, in disguise, as 3,000 people attended the Congress of the People in Kliptown, near Johannesburg. As the Freedom Charter was read out, everyone cheered. The police were there, too, but on the first day, they simply observed the proceedings. On the second day of the Congress, though, the police attacked. They took the names of every person there. "The people responded magnificently by loudly singing Nkosi Sikelel' iAfrika," said Nelson, who escaped unnoticed by authorities.

It would be almost a year before the Congress of the People finally adopted the Freedom Charter. Of course, the white government disapproved of the revolutionary document. On December 5, 1956, it showed the degree of its displeasure. That day, police conducted a coordinated set of raids on the homes of ANC leaders.

They arrived at Nelson's home at dawn and arrested him for treason. Before the week was out, police had arrested 155 other people under the same charge, including Nelson's friends Walter Sisulu and Oliver Tambo.

Chapter 5
The "Black Pimpernel"

In 1955, the bad news was that Nelson Mandela, Oliver Tambo, Walter Sisulu, and more than 150 others found themselves in Johannesburg Prison. The good news was that this was the first time they'd been legally allowed to meet together since 1952! The government that had forbidden their gatherings had now thrown them all "under one roof for what became the largest and longest unbanned meeting in years," said Nelson. The men took advantage of their time together in prison to hold discussion groups, to educate each other, to share ideas, and to plan future protest activities. They sang freedom songs, danced, and "felt the power of the great cause that linked us all together."

Prison, Protests, and Public Outrage

After two weeks in jail, Nelson and the others were transported to a makeshift courthouse in a nearby military building. They traveled in a convoy, or group, of police vans, surrounded by soldiers. Supporters lined the streets, cheering loudly as the vehicles passed. "The trip became a triumphal procession," said Nelson. Inside the courtroom, more supporters cheered and chanted, creating a mood of celebration, rather than punishment.

It took two days for prosecutors to read the charges against the 156 accused. All of them were charged with high treason and conspiracy to overthrow the government of South Africa. The accusations stemmed from their involvement with the Defiance Campaign, the Freedom Charter, the Congress of the People, and the Sophiatown protests.

Finally, just before Christmas 1956, the prisoners were released on bail. Three weeks later, they returned to court for initial hearings. In the end, the trial was to last four years. During that time, the prosecution presented 12,000 documents and 150 witnesses. In 1957, charges against 61 accused, including Oliver Tambo, were dropped. The following year, another 65 charges were dropped, leaving just 30 activists—including Nelson and Walter—on trial for treason. All were free on bail until they took the witness stand in 1960.

Meanwhile, in 1958, a new, even more oppressive government took power in South Africa. (Again, blacks, Indians, and other people of color had not been allowed to vote.) Under what was now called *groot,* or "grand apartheid," this government enacted even stricter laws against non-whites. It created "homelands," or reserves, for black Africans. These were designed to further separate blacks from whites, and to keep the blacks in poverty. Until now, just the black men had to carry passes to allow them into white areas. Now, the government extended the pass laws to black women. Anyone caught without a pass would be arrested.

Second Family

In 1957, Nelson Mandela met Nomzamo Winifred Madikizela ("Winnie"). She was a Xhosa woman born in Bizana, about 155 miles (250 km) from Nelson's childhood home of Qunu. In Johannesburg, Winnie worked as a social worker. She was educated, beautiful, and politically aware. For Nelson, it was love at first sight when he met her.

Winnie and Nelson Mandela in an undated photo, probably taken in the late 1950s.

Despite the age difference—Winnie was 16 years younger than Nelson—they married a year after they met, on June 14, 1958. At the time, Nelson was in the middle of his treason trial, and Winnie stood by him through it.

The couple had two daughters. Zenani ("Zeni") was born early in 1959, and her little sister, Zindziswa ("Zindzi"), came along two years later. Unlike Nelson's first wife, Winnie supported her husband's cause. She was politically active throughout her life. Still, she and Nelson separated in 1992, and divorced four years later.

Children in QwaQwa, one of the ten "homelands," also known as bantustans, in South Africa established by the government during apartheid. Although the stated purpose of the homelands was to set up "independent" black African states, they were still under South African rule. The effect of them was to further isolate black Africans from white South Africans and to deny them voting rights and other benefits of being full-fledged South Africans. When apartheid was abolished in the 1990s, the homelands were reunited with the rest of South Africa.

THE ARCHITECT OF APARTHEID

Hendrik Verwoerd was born in Amsterdam, the Netherlands, in 1901, but his family moved to South Africa when he was a toddler. As a young adult, he lived and studied in Germany, Britain, and the United States. He returned to South Africa in 1928, and taught sociology, psychology, and social work.

In 1937, Verwoerd became the editor of *Die Transvaler*, a daily newspaper dedicated to building up the National Party of South Africa. When the National Party won the 1948 election and formed the government of South Africa, Verwoerd became a senator. Two years later, he was appointed Minister of Native Affairs.

In that role, he was responsible for creating apartheid laws—laws that said every person in South Africa was to be classified by race, that different races were to live in separate parts of a city, and that black men and women were to carry passes to give them permission to enter white areas of the city. He also created laws forbidding non-whites from entering whites-only parks, cinemas, beaches, swimming pools, buses, hospitals, and other public buildings.

Because of this work, Hendrik Verwoerd has been called the "architect of apartheid." Later, when he became prime minister of South Africa, his government developed even stricter apartheid laws, further separating whites and non-whites.

In 1960, a white farmer tried to assassinate Verwoerd. He failed, but six years later, a middle-aged man of mixed race succeeded in stabbing and killing him.

Instead of heeding the world's calls for an end to the cruelty in South Africa, the ruling National Party did the opposite.

A year later, a new protest group splintered off from the ANC. It was called the Pan-Africanist Congress (PAC). Members of this group believed in "a government of the Africans by the Africans and for the Africans." In the PAC's vision of Africa, there were no whites, or Indians, or anyone other than black Africans. While the group never gained the strength of the mainstream ANC, it was responsible for one memorable, and horrible, moment in South Africa's history.

In 1960, the ANC began organizing an anti-pass campaign that was to last three months. Rather than joining the ANC's efforts, the PAC decided to stage its own campaign, which started 10 days before the ANC's protest was scheduled to begin. On March 21, the PAC urged black men and women to march to their local police stations without their passes, knowing they would be arrested for not carrying the required documents.

At one police station, in the township of Sharpeville, which was about 45 miles (70 km) south of Johannesburg, thousands of people gathered. That afternoon, police opened fire on the crowd, killing 69 people and injuring hundreds of others.

An officer stands near the body of a demonstrator killed by police gunfire during what came to be known as the Sharpeville Massacre.

THE ORIGINAL PIMPERNEL

When Nelson Mandela was in hiding, but still active within the ANC, the media called him "the Black Pimpernel." That nickname was a play on the title of a famous book, *The Scarlet Pimpernel*, written in 1905. The author, Baroness Emma Orczy, was born in Hungary but spent most of her life in England.

Set during the French Revolution, the book tells the adventures of a wealthy Englishman, Sir Percy, who rescues political prisoners who have been sentenced to death. To torment his enemies, this hero leaves a picture of a flower, a scarlet pimpernel, at the scene of every rescue. Authorities call the man the Scarlet Pimpernel, because they don't know his true identity. Efforts to capture Sir Percy fail because he is an escape artist and a master of disguise who has a secret network of supporters helping him with his rescue efforts. Sound familiar?

This has since been called the "Sharpeville Massacre," and it made international news headlines.

The ANC called for a national day of mourning on March 28. On that day, and for several days afterward, hundreds of thousands of people took to the streets across South Africa to protest the police brutality. Nelson burned his pass in public, in front of international news photographers.

Nelson Mandela burns his passbook as a public sign of protest and defiance in the wake of the Sharpeville Massacre in 1960.

Inspiring Nelson: Walter Sisulu

One person who influenced Nelson Mandela as he became more politically active was Walter Sisulu.

Like Nelson, Walter was a Xhosa man born in the Transkei region of South Africa. Walter's mother was a black servant who worked for white people. His father was a white government employee. Walter's parents never married. Walter was born in 1912. He quit school when he was 14 and held a variety of jobs to help support his family.

While in his late teens, Walter worked in the gold mines. He also met the leader of one of the local labor unions. These two experiences sparked his passion for politics and the fight for equal rights.

Walter joined the African National Congress (ANC) in 1940, co-founding the Youth League four years later, and *Umkhonto we Sizwe* (MK), the ANC's militant wing, in 1962. He rose within the ranks of the ANC, eventually becoming its leader.

When Walter married his wife, Albertina, in 1944, Nelson was best man at the wedding. Walter and Albertina had five children and adopted four more. He died on May 5, 2003.

The wedding of Walter and Albertina Sisulu, in 1944, was attended by a host of friends, family, and fellow ANC leaders. In this photo, taken at the Bantu Men's Social Centre in Johannesburg, South Africa, Walter and Albertina are standing at the center, holding a bouquet. Looking over their shoulders is Walter's sister, Rosabella. Standing next to Walter, to the left as viewed by the camera, is Nelson Mandela's first wife, Evelyn, and to the left of her is Nelson. On Albertina's right is another of Nelson's good friends and ANC compatriots, Anton Lembede.

About 50,000 people protested in Cape Town, and riots broke out in other centers. The United Nations, the United States, and Britain called on the government of South Africa to stop its oppressive tactics.

The Fight Continues

Instead of heeding the world's calls for an end to the cruelty in South Africa, the ruling National Party did the opposite. It cracked down even more severely on activists. On March 30, 1960, the government declared a state of emergency, meaning police could arrest anyone they suspected of any rebellious activity. Nelson, who was out on bail in the ongoing treason trial, was re-arrested that day. He was held in Pretoria Prison until the state of emergency was lifted five months later. By then, more than 2,000 people had been arrested.

When the state of emergency ended, the treason trial against the remaining 30 accused continued. Nelson and Walter were among those still on trial. Finally, on March 29, 1961, all 30 people were finally found not guilty of all charges.

Instead of celebrating, though, Nelson immediately went into hiding, knowing he was a government target. He disguised his appearance. He grew a beard and began stooping and mumbling, rather than standing tall. He posed as a gardener or chauffeur, so he would look like just another invisible black worker. He moved from safe house to safe house around the country.

Secretly, he and Walter continued to hold ANC meetings, to plan further protests and demonstrations. The media dubbed Nelson the "Black Pimpernel" because, like the "Scarlet Pimpernel" in the famous novel of the same name, Nelson was an outlaw on the lam. The police knew he was out there organizing ANC activities, but they could not find him. For the public, Nelson became a most thrilling character.

He was a charismatic leader in disguise, fooling the police and government, while continuing his mission of promoting freedom and equality for all. To add to the mystique, Nelson even called newspapers, anonymously, with tips about the ANC's upcoming protests and demonstrations.

When the government learned that the ANC was planning a huge three-day strike for late May in 1961, it made it clear that it would not tolerate such activity. On the first day of the proposed protest, the prime minister called out armed soldiers in armored vehicles to crush anyone who dared speak out. ANC leaders canceled the rest of the strike. They feared it would end up being a bloodbath, or massacre, by the military. For Nelson, this threat of government violence strengthened his belief that nonviolence was no longer the way to go for the ANC. "*Sebatana ha se bokwe ka diatla*," he said. "The attacks of the wild beast cannot be averted with only bare hands."

With that, Nelson, Walter, and members of the ANC and other protest groups created a new, more aggressive, organization called *Umkhonto*

ᴉdela and his ANC colleagues realized their nonviolent
ᴉg the government wasn't working, they launched
ᴡe ("MK"). This group used guerrilla warfare tactics to fight
they used a series of violent hit-and-run attacks to further
ᴉllas, who are usually revolutionaries fighting established,
ᴉilitary foes, typically travel in small, highly mobile groups
ᴇmy territory against a large army or government. They
ᴉt of surprise, and they use strategies such as ambush,
ᴉbings to confuse, tire, and distract their enemies.

we Sizwe ("MK"), or "Spear of the Nation." With
Nelson as its first Commander-in-Chief, this
group furthered its cause by taking up arms
and using sabotage (destroying or damaging
something on purpose, usually to achieve a
military or political goal). In December 1961,
MK began a series of bombings of power plants
and government offices around the country.
The goal was to cripple government buildings
and activities without hurting any people.

Early in 1962, the South African government
and military set out to find and capture
members of MK. Somehow, Nelson managed
to avoid arrest and leave South Africa for the
first time in his life. For the next seven months,
he traveled to other African nations, meeting
with colleagues and studying guerrilla warfare
tactics in other countries. He also visited
London, England, to meet with politicians and
supporters—and to sightsee!

Friends in London tried to convince Nelson
to stay in England, to stay away from South
Africa. "A leader stays with his people," was
Nelson's reply.

Freedom Fighter Loses His Freedom

Days after he returned to South Africa in the summer of 1962, the police finally caught up with Nelson. They found out he was at a meeting, lay in wait for him, and arrested him on his way home. Nelson was charged with inciting, or convincing, workers to strike and leaving the country without a passport.

Nelson did not hire a lawyer. Instead, he represented himself in court, wearing traditional Xhosa attire. He said:

> *"I had chosen traditional dress to emphasize the symbolism that I was a black African walking into a white man's court. I was literally carrying on my back the history, culture, and heritage of my people."*

During his travels outside of South Africa in 1962, Nelson Mandela received military training in other nations. He is shown here, second from left, with a group of rebel fighters during the Algerian War of Independence, in which the former French colony in North Africa achieved its independence.

"*Whatever sentence Your Worship sees fit to impose upon me for the crime for which I have been convicted before this court, may it rest assured that when my sentence has been completed, I will still be moved, as men are always moved, by their consciences. I will still be moved by my dislike of the race discrimination against my people ... to take up again, as best I can, the struggle for the removal of those injustices until they are finally abolished once and for all.*"

Nelson Mandela, speaking in his own defense, November 7, 1962

During the trial, which lasted almost a month, the ANC launched a "Free Mandela" campaign. Supporters protested on Nelson's behalf, wrote the slogan on the sides of buildings, and packed into the courtroom to offer encouragement.

The prosecutor called more than 100 witnesses against Nelson, who didn't even try to fight the charges. After all, he was guilty! When it was his turn to speak, rather than arguing in his own defense, Nelson gave a one-hour speech about the importance of peace and freedom. "I wanted to explain to the court how and why I had become the man I was, why I had done what I had done, and why, if given the chance, I would do it again," he said.

At the end of the trial, Nelson was sentenced to five years in prison, the harshest sentence ever given for a political offense.

Eight months later, while Nelson was still in jail, the government filed even more charges against him. These new accusations stemmed from Nelson's involvement with MK. This time, the charges were much more serious—and this time, the penalty could be death.

Nelson Mandela spent the bulk of his prison term at the maximum-security prison on Robben Island, off the coast of South Africa. The conditions at Robben Island were harsh, and for most of his time there, Nelson did hard labor at a lime quarry. Today the prison is, like the rest of the island, a historic site that is open to the public. This was Nelson's cell.

Chapter 6
Prisoner Number 466/64

Just after Nelson Mandela was arrested in the summer of 1962, police also raided the safe house where he had been staying. The house was located in a suburb of Johannesburg called Rivonia—and all the MK leaders were there the night police stormed in. All nine of them were arrested. In the house, police also found Nelson's diary documenting his trip abroad, along with plans for MK's future guerrilla activities and instructions for bomb making. They had enough evidence to charge Nelson and the others with sabotage and conspiracy to overthrow the government. The trial, which became known as "the Rivonia Trial," was the most important court case in apartheid history.

Holding Court

The trial against Nelson Mandela, Walter Sisulu, and the other eight accused began on October 9, 1963. The men knew they would be found guilty on all charges and expected the judge to order the maximum penalty—execution. After some initial stalling, the prosecution finally began presenting its case in December. The trial dragged on for about seven months. Lawyers questioned 173 witnesses and presented thousands of maps, notes, and other documents as evidence against the men.

Nelson's prison number has become a symbol of the man himself and the trademark of the campaign he launched against AIDS in 2002. Pronounced "four-double-six six-four," it was also the title of a series of concerts that raised money for the AIDS campaign.

Nelson, who was 45 years old at the time, took the stand on April 20, 1964. His mother and his wife Winnie were there to hear his testimony, as were hundreds of other supporters. Nelson felt he had nothing to lose, so, rather than speaking in his own defense, he gave one of the most passionate, and memorable, speeches of his life. He spoke for four hours—about his own history, why he joined the ANC, and the inequalities, indignities, and injustices faced by black Africans in their own country. Thanks to the international media who attended the Rivonia Trial, Nelson's speech, known as the "I Am Prepared to Die" speech, was published around the world.

"During my lifetime I have dedicated myself to this struggle of the African people. I have fought against white domination, and I have fought against black domination. I have cherished the ideal of a democratic and free society in which all persons live together in harmony and with equal opportunities. It is an ideal which I hope to live for and to achieve. But if needs be, it is an ideal for which I am prepared to die."

Nelson Mandela, in his "I Am Prepared to Die" speech, April 20, 1964

Nelson truly was willing to die in the name of freedom, but thanks to protests from international leaders, and a brilliant legal team, he did not have to. In the end, the judge did not impose the death sentence.

Instead, in a surprise announcement on June 11, 1964, he sentenced Nelson and six others, including Walter, to life in prison. (One of the accused men was found not guilty.)

Later that night, in secret, with a heavy police escort, the inmates were flown to Robben Island, site of a maximum-security jail for political prisoners. Located about 4 miles (6.5 km) off the west coast of South Africa, this cold, rocky island prison would be Nelson's home for the next 18 years.

Maximum Security, Minimum Privileges

When they arrived at Robben Island, the men were issued prison uniforms—shorts, a thin shirt and jacket, and shoes without socks. They were also issued numbers. Nelson became prisoner number 466/64, meaning he was the 466th prisoner to be jailed at Robben Island in 1964.

The men were then segregated based on skin color, and treated differently depending on skin color. Blacks, of course, received the harshest treatment. "You have no idea of the cruelty of man against man until you have been in a South African prison with white warders and black prisoners," said Nelson.

Inmates were also divided according to their level of influence in the outside community. Nelson and other leaders were kept apart from the general prison population, to make sure

Nelson Mandela, Walter Sisulu, and other prisoners in the Rivonia Trial defiantly give the ANC salute through the bars of a prison bus as they are transported between court and jail.

they could not organize, rally, or communicate with others.

They were monitored by racist, white-skinned armed guards with attack dogs. They were regularly insulted, beaten, and punished for any little misstep. They lived by a strict schedule that dictated when they got up, when they ate, when they could wash (only in cold water), when they went to work, and when they went to bed.

They were forbidden to speak to each other. They were only allowed two visitors and two letters a year. They were not allowed news from the outside world. They ate mashed corn, boiled corn, and corn porridge. They had to sleep with the lights on.

Nelson lived in a damp, 6-foot- (2-meter-) wide cell with a bucket instead of a toilet. He slept on the floor on a thin straw mat, with

three flimsy blankets for warmth. He often wore his clothes to bed to help combat the cold. He had one small pleasure in his cell—a small, barred window that gave him a view of the prison courtyard.

In this undated photo of Nelson Mandela at Robben Island, he is shown repairing an article of his clothing. For years, black prisoners were allowed only to wear shorts during their work at the quarry. After years of pressuring authorities for improvements in prison conditions, Nelson and other prisoners were eventually allowed to wear long pants.

HARD LABOR

Limestone is a light-colored rock composed of calcium and other minerals. It is often crushed to make cement and concrete, and is used as a construction material for roads and buildings. Nelson Mandela hammered limestone in a quarry for 13 years. Because it is a white stone, the sun reflected off the walls of the quarry, permanently damaging his eyes. He worked for three years before he was allowed to wear sunglasses. Pounding rock all day was strenuous work, which damaged Nelson's back as he aged. In addition, the limestone dust got into his lungs, causing him breathing problems.

During the day, the inmates worked. Of course, the black workers were assigned the worst tasks. Nelson's job was to break stones into fine gravel with a hammer. At first, he pounded rocks in the prison courtyard. After six months, he was transferred to a nearby lime quarry, where he did the same thing. It was hard labor, but Nelson enjoyed the walk to and from the quarry every day. There, too, he was allowed to talk to the other inmates, a group that included Walter and the others from the Rivonia Trial. The men worked in the quarry for 13 years.

During his time at Robben Island, Nelson challenged everything. He became a leader and spokesperson for the inmates, representing them in meetings with the guards and with the International Red Cross. He was always respectful and polite to guards, even when he demanded that things change. Over the years, he lobbied for sunglasses for quarry workers, long pants for the black inmates (they were the only ones forced to wear shorts), warmer clothes, and better food. Gradually, with the

FAMILY MATTERS

In the spring of 1968, Nelson saw his mother for the first time since the Rivonia Trial. She visited him at Robben Island, along with two of Nelson's children and his sister. Because they had come so far to see Nelson, the guards allowed them to stay 45 minutes, rather than the usual 30. A few weeks after the visit, Nelson's mother died suddenly of a heart attack. Less than a year later, Nelson got more bad news. His eldest son Thembi, 25, had been killed in a car accident. "It left a hole in my heart that can never be filled," said Nelson of the tragedy. He was not allowed to attend either funeral.

help of the Red Cross, conditions improved, and some of the rules relaxed.

Eventually, the men were permitted to post photos in their cells. They were allowed to talk to each other. The number of visitors and letters increased to one a month, instead of two a year. One of the greatest victories for the inmates was the day they were granted study privileges. Many of them started taking correspondence courses in such subjects as English, history, geography, and math. They began teaching each other what they learned. "We became our own faculty, with our own professors, our own curriculum, our own courses," said Nelson, who resumed his law studies while at Robben Island.

Throughout the early 1960s, political prisoners from a variety of other organizations continued to arrive at Robben Island. The commanding officer at the jail put all the leaders of all the groups in Nelson's cellblock. He thought it would be easier to keep an eye on them if they were all in one place. Instead, it allowed inmates to learn about each other's organizations and to start working together. They figured out ways to communicate with each other and with inmates in other parts of the prison. They left tiny, secret notes on discarded matchboxes, in food bins, under dirty dishes, and under toilet seats. They also found ways to smuggle messages to the outside world.

"We supported each other and gained strength from each other," said Nelson. "We would fight inside as we had fought outside."

By the early 1970s, life at Robben Island was almost bearable. The food had improved, and the men were allowed to meet pretty much any time they chose. They played cards and board games, and even put on plays and concerts. They had regular Sunday church services. At the quarry, they socialized more than they worked. It got to the point, said Nelson, that "the inmates seemed to be running the prison, not the authorities."

Nelson Mandela and his friend and ANC colleague Walter Sisulu (right) are shown talking in the prison yard at Robben Island. With the eventual relaxing of prison rules forbidding inmates from talking, Nelson and Walter were able to meet without fear of punishment.

"Free Mandela"

In 1975, Nelson secretly began writing his life story. Every night, instead of sleeping, he wrote pages and pages of memories. Another inmate, who had the odd ability to write in teeny-tiny letters,

Nelson Mandela and Walter Sisulu in the prison yard. 1966

then transcribed Nelson's long pages onto a single small sheet of paper. These small pages were later smuggled out of the prison, and eventually they formed the basis of Nelson's autobiography, *Long Walk to Freedom*.

By the mid 1970s, too, the men had been permitted to grow a vegetable garden. This was one of Nelson's greatest joys. It was also a great hiding place. In the garden, Nelson buried the original, full-sized pages of his life story. In 1976, though, during a building project, guards unearthed some of the papers. Nelson managed to destroy the rest, but he, Walter, and a third inmate were punished for writing the forbidden documents. They were denied study privileges for the rest of their time at Robben Island. That turned out to be four more years.

During those final years, though, the inmates' lives continued to improve in other ways. Their time hammering rocks at the lime quarry finally came to an end in 1977. In addition, they were allowed newspapers, movies, and recreation equipment. They got a ping-pong table and volleyball gear, and they set up a tennis court. (To keep in shape, Nelson had practiced his boxing routine and had done

INTERNATIONAL DISAPPROVAL

Sometimes, the leaders of some countries—especially wealthy countries like the United States, Canada, and Britain—want to force leaders of other countries to make changes. To do that, they may impose economic or trade sanctions. That means they stop doing business with the offending country. That in turn harms the economy, or financial health, of that country. Usually, sanctions are put in place to force leaders to make changes related to human rights and democracy.

pushups, deep knee bends, and jogging-in-place the whole time he'd been at Robben Island.) The inmates finally had healthy food to eat and good books to read.

In the meantime, the rest of the world—inside and outside South Africa—had virtually forgotten about Nelson Mandela. Many countries had eased their economic sanctions on the country, and there was a whole new generation of black leaders drawing attention away from the older, imprisoned ANC organizers. These up-and-coming activists, mostly students, started what they called the "black consciousness movement" to combat apartheid, which was still the rule in South Africa.

Because of these young activists, apartheid—and the cruelty of South Africa's leaders—once again made international headlines in 1976. In June of that year, students banded together to protest new language laws. The new rules said that half the courses in South African schools and universities were to be taught in Afrikaans. This made the students angry because

Students in Soweto protest against the government's apartheid policies. These protests, which came to be known as the "Soweto Uprising," were triggered by language laws that put Afrikaans, which most blacks considered the language of the white oppressors, on a level with English. Today, the anniversary of the first day of the uprising, June 16, is South Africa's National Youth Day. On this day, cultural and legal issues related to young people are recognized.

Afrikaans was the language of the people who had created apartheid.

On June 16, more than 10,000 students and schoolchildren staged a protest in Soweto, just outside Johannesburg. Police swarmed the scene, using tear gas, attack dogs, and guns to try to stop the demonstration. They opened fire into the crowds of young people. By the end of the day, police had killed at least 25 people, including children. (This is the "official" death toll. Other estimates say up to 200 people died that day, and some estimates put the number higher still.)

THE MAN ON THE OUTSIDE

Unlike Nelson Mandela and other ANC leaders, Oliver Tambo managed to stay out of jail during the anti-apartheid struggle. In 1959, the ANC smuggled him out of South Africa, so he could continue the group's activities from a safe place. For years, he organized anti-apartheid protests throughout Africa and Europe. He also successfully lobbied governments around the world to boycott South Africa. In 1980, Oliver started the "Free Mandela" campaign, which quickly spread around the globe. This campaign, along with Oliver's other international work, gathered so much support that the South African government eventually released Nelson and other political prisoners. Oliver returned to South Africa in 1990, the year apartheid ended. He died in Johannesburg three years later.

This photo, taken in the early 1980s, shows ANC leader Oliver Tambo (right) meeting with the prime minister of the Netherlands, Dries van Agt. During this time, Tambo, who was Nelson Mandela's friend and former law partner, launched the "Free Mandela" campaign, which made Nelson the central focus of anti-apartheid efforts around the world.

The massacre prompted months of riots, violence, and protests across the nation. News of the "Soweto Uprising" spread worldwide. The United Nations and Britain once again called for economic sanctions against South Africa.

Conditions in the country continued to deteriorate over the next few years. By 1980, even white South Africans were questioning the government's tactics and calling for change. Oliver Tambo, who was living in exile in Zambia at the time, came up with a brilliant idea to draw attention to the cause. He launched a "Free Mandela" campaign to personalize the apartheid struggle, to put a face on it.

The *Johannesburg Sunday Post* printed an article about the campaign on March 9, 1980. The large headline in the newspaper read "Free Mandela." Inside was a petition that people could sign to demand the release of Nelson and the other political prisoners.

International media soon picked up on the "Free Mandela" story. The campaign—with Nelson's face on it—spread around the globe. Nelson became the most famous political prisoner in the world.

To government leaders in South Africa, Nelson was still considered a traitor. They couldn't just give in to international pressure and let him walk free. Instead, as a sort of compromise designed to save face, the government transferred Nelson to a nicer prison in 1982.

Pollsmoor Prison, located in Cape Town, was luxury living compared to Robben Island. Walter and the others who had been convicted

in the Rivonia Trial joined Nelson there. Because the world was now watching, the government had to treat these men with care and respect.

Free South Africa

As efforts to free Nelson continued, so did the protests, boycotts, and sabotage in South Africa at large. In 1983, hundreds of organizations—churches, student groups, trade unions, ethnic organizations, even sports teams—banded together to form the United Democratic Front (UDF). This group adopted the ANC's Freedom Charter as its mandate, and its goal was to end apartheid once and for all.

To try to divide the group, the government granted certain rights to Indians and other non-white groups, but not to blacks. The UDF rejected this arrangement, demanding equal rights for all South Africans. By 1985, the UDF had about three million members and had stepped up its protest activity. One of its most famous leaders was Archbishop Desmond Tutu, who had won the 1984 Nobel Peace Prize.

By this time, too, MK—the violent branch of the ANC Nelson had co-founded—had been revived. It began a campaign of bombing, violence, and sabotage in the name of ending apartheid.

To try to appease the anti-apartheid organizations, and to honor international calls to "Free Mandela," South African President P. W. Botha offered the world's most famous inmate a deal. He said Nelson could go free if he agreed to publically renounce, or reject, violence as a tool to fight apartheid.

"*I am not a violent man. It was only ... when all other forms of resistance were no longer open to us, that we turned to armed struggle.... Let [President Botha] renounce violence. Let him say that he will dismantle apartheid.... Let him free all who have been imprisoned, banished or exiled for their opposition to apartheid. Let him guarantee free political activity so that people may decide who will govern them. I cherish my own freedom dearly, but I care even more for your freedom.... I cannot and will not give any undertaking at a time when I and you, the people, are not free. Your freedom and mine cannot be separated. I will return.*"

Nelson Mandela, February 10, 1985,
as read by his daughter Zindzi

Nelson refused, saying he would only accept unconditional release. He wrote a statement in which he declared his refusal to gain his personal freedom at the expense of the fight for freedom for all South Africans. Read by his daughter Zindzi at a massive event called

Nelson Mandela's daughter Zindzi is carried to the stage by supporters during a 1985 rally in Soweto. There, she read a statement from her father, declaring his refusal to bargain for his freedom with a government that would deny freedom for all South Africans.

Rally in Soweto, it was the first time the public had heard Nelson's words in 21 years.

Throughout 1985, rioting, boycotts, and demonstrations raged across the country. In the summer, the government declared a state of emergency. By the time it was lifted nine months later, another 750 people had died, and police had arrested more than 8,000 others.

As its citizens protested at home, the government of South Africa was also losing respect on the world stage. Many nations refused to do business with the country until conditions changed. In 1988, the United Nations called for Nelson's unconditional release.

Displaying crosses, the ANC flag, and pictures of Nelson Mandela, thousands rally in early 1986 at a sports stadium in South Africa. The memorial service for victims of police shootings also served as a bold demonstration against the South African government at a time when oppostion to apartheid was gaining momentum in South Africa and around the world.

Happy 70th Birthday!

In honor of Nelson Mandela's 70th birthday, and to raise global awareness about apartheid in South Africa, almost 100 celebrities staged a 12-hour concert at Wembley Stadium in London, England. Held on June 11, 1988, the concert had a variety of names—The Nelson Mandela 70th Birthday Tribute, Freedomfest, the Free Mandela Concert, and Mandela Day.

Singers, bands, actors, comedians, and other celebrities entertained more than 75,000 people at the stadium. Another 600 million people in 67 countries watched the concert on TV.

Among the acts on stage were Sting, Eurythmics, Brian Adams, the Bee Gees, UB40, Whitney Houston, Stevie Wonder, Phil Collins, Simple Minds, and Dire Straits.

In 1990, a second concert took place at Wembley Stadium to celebrate Nelson's release from prison. When Nelson walked on stage, the tens of thousands of people in the audience gave him an eight-minute-long standing ovation.

That same year, dozens of musicians and international celebrities threw a massive 70th birthday party in Nelson's honor. Staged at Wembley Stadium in London, England, the "Free Nelson Mandela Concert," as it was called, put Nelson—and apartheid—into the international spotlight once again. The government of South Africa could no longer ignore the world's pleas to free Nelson.

By this time, Nelson was deep in private negotiations with officials trying to figure out how to release him while saving face for the government. International negotiators were working toward the same goal.

By this time, too, Nelson's health had become a concern. He underwent prostate surgery, had high blood pressure, and was treated for

Residents of Soweto celebrate the news of Nelson Mandela's freedom on February 11, the day of his release from Victor Verster Prison.

tuberculosis. For the government, "the only thing worse than a free Mandela is a dead Mandela," announced London's *Sunday Times* newspaper. The international icon had to be well cared for—the world would never forgive South Africa if its most famous resident died in jail.

As a gesture of good will, in December 1988 the government moved Nelson to what he called "a halfway house between prison and freedom"—a private cottage on the campus of Victor Verster Prison, 37 miles (60 km) east of Cape Town.

There, Nelson received many visits from family and friends and continued his secret meetings with government officials. The biggest step in negotiating his release, though, came through a change in South Africa's leadership. Early in 1989, President Botha suffered a stroke and was no longer able to head the National Party. In September of that year, the country elected a new president, F. W. de Klerk, whose goal was "to bring justice to everybody" and to end apartheid.

True to his word, a month after the election, de Klerk released Walter Sisulu and the other Rivonia inmates from Pollsmoor Prison. Four months later, he announced he was abolishing all apartheid laws. All political prisoners, including Nelson Mandela, were to be unconditionally freed.

Chapter 7
President and Statesman

On February 11, 1990, Nelson Mandela walked out of Victor Verster Prison, arm in arm with his wife Winnie. Thousands of supporters and hundreds of reporters, photographers, and television cameras greeted him. "When I was among the crowd, I raised my right fist and there was a roar," remembered Nelson. "As I finally walked through those gates ... I felt—even at the age of 71—that my life was beginning anew. My 10,000 days of imprisonment were over."

Amandla! (Power!)

On the day of his release from prison, Nelson made his first public appearance in almost 30 years. Then he got down to work. South Africa

A jubilant Nelson Mandela and his wife, Winnie, raise their fists in the ANC salute as Nelson leaves Victor Verster Prison on February 11, 1990.

THE TROUBLE WITH WINNIE

In 1962, four years after she married Nelson, Winnie Mandela found herself alone. Her husband had been jailed and would remain imprisoned for the next 27 years. When she was permitted, Winnie visited him in prison and wrote him letters. She fully supported Nelson and the anti-apartheid movement and continued the fight while he was behind bars.

Because of that, she, too, was targeted by police, arrested many times, questioned, monitored, and generally harassed. At one point, she spent more than a year in jail in solitary confinement. She was tortured. Later, police forcibly moved her out of Johannesburg and placed her under house arrest in a remote town.

In Nelson's absence, Winnie became the face of the anti-apartheid fight around the world. She was called the "Mother of the Nation" because of her commitment to the cause—but there was a dark side to that commitment. Winnie was known to punish black Africans who supported apartheid. Her bodyguards, nicknamed the "Mandela United Football Club," were violent toughs who did her bidding.

In a 1986 speech, Winnie publically stated that she supported the practice of "necklacing," or setting fire to a gasoline-soaked tire while it was around someone's neck. Later, she was accused of ordering the kidnapping and murder of a 14-year-old boy she suspected was a spy.

By the time Nelson was released from prison in 1990, Winnie had become involved in a romantic relationship with another man. She may have been at her husband's side as he walked out of prison, but their marriage was all but over. The couple separated in 1992, divorcing in 1996.

In 1997, a government commission found Winnie guilty of "gross violations of human rights," related to the violence committed by her bodyguards.

was still a country divided. Violence between blacks and whites, and between different ethnic organizations, continued.

Nelson began working with President de Klerk to draw up a new constitution for South Africa, one that decreed that all citizens were equal. A constitution is a document that states how a country will be governed. Nelson and de Klerk didn't agree on everything as they designed the new document, but they agreed that the violence tearing the country apart had to stop. They knew that a new constitution would help reach that goal. Finally, in 1993, the government accepted a draft, or proposed version, of a new constitution. The final document took effect three years later.

Meanwhile, in 1991, Nelson had been elected president of the ANC. In 1993, he and President de Klerk were awarded the Nobel Peace Prize for their efforts to create peace and equality in South Africa. The biggest step toward that equality came a year later when, in April 1994, South Africa held its first-ever fully democratic elections.

Millions of black Africans—including Nelson—voted for the first time in their lives. The ANC won 62.6 percent of the vote. As ANC leader, Nelson, at age 75, became South

Nelson Mandela casts his ballot in South Africa's first fully democratic elections.

AMCP

ANC

DP

AFRICAN MODERATES CONGRESS PARTY

AFRICAN NATIONAL CONGRESS

DEMOCRATIC PARTY –
DEMOKRATIESE PARTY

The ballot for South Africa's first fully democratic elections had 18 political parties on it. The African National Congress (ANC), represented by Nelson Mandela, appeared on the 12th line of the ballot.

Africa's first black president. To illustrate his government's commitment to unity, he named former president de Klerk as one of his deputy presidents. He even invited his former prison guards to his inauguration ceremony.

That day, May 10, 1994, he spoke to a crowd of 100,000 cheering supporters.

"The time for the healing of the wounds has come," Nelson said. "The moment to bridge the chasms that divide us has come. The time to build is upon us." He further proclaimed:

"We shall build the society in which all South Africans, both black and white, will be able to walk tall, without any fear in their hearts, assured of their inalienable right to human dignity—a rainbow nation at peace with itself and the world."

As president, Nelson focused on resolving conflicts among the various South African ethnic groups, putting a stop to violence, and rebuilding the country and its economy. He also worked toward restoring South Africa's reputation as a respected nation within the world at large.

Nelson and his government made mistakes along the way, and they certainly didn't solve all of South Africa's problems. Still, they made great strides toward democracy, stability, and equal rights for all.

When Nelson took the office of president, he said he would only serve one term as his nation's leader. Then he would turn the ANC—and running the country—over to younger people. True to his word, the 81-year-old leader

"We understand it, still, that there is no easy road to freedom. We know it well that none of us acting alone can achieve success. We must therefore act together as a united people, for national reconciliation, for nation building, for the birth of a new world.

Let there be justice for all. Let there be peace for all. Let there be work, bread, water and salt for all. Let each know that for each the body, the mind and the soul have been freed to fulfill themselves.

Never, never and never again shall it be that this beautiful land will again experience the oppression of one by another and suffer the indignity of being the skunk of the world.

Let freedom reign.

The sun shall never set on so glorious a human achievement!

God bless Africa!"

Excerpt from Nelson Mandela's Inaugural Celebration speech, May 10, 1994

resigned from politics in June 1999, when his term as president ended.

"A Hero of Our Time"

Having divorced Winnie in 1996, Nelson married his third wife, Graça Machel, in 1998. When he stepped down as president, the couple retired to Qunu, the village of his youth—but that didn't mean Nelson stopped working. He

NOT JUST FOR PEACE

In 1993, Nelson Mandela and F. W. de Klerk won the Nobel Peace Prize. That same year, seven other people won Nobel Prizes—two in physics, two in chemistry, two in medicine, and one in literature.

Since 1901, achievements in all these categories have been honored with the prize named for Alfred Nobel, a wealthy Swedish poet, playwright, and scientist. When he died in 1896, Alfred left money in his will to establish the annual awards. Each Nobel Prize winner gets a medal, diploma, and cash.

Other Nobel Peace Prize winners include the following: U.S. President Barack Obama (2009); former U.S. Vice President Al Gore (2007); Tibetan spiritual leader the Dalai Lama (1989); Catholic nun and advocate for the poor and helpless, Mother Teresa (1979); and U.S. civil rights leader Martin Luther King Jr. (1964).

continued to speak out about human rights, peace, health care, and education, in South Africa and around the world. He raised money for the Nelson Mandela Children's Fund and established two more charitable foundations in his name. In 2002, he launched an AIDS awareness and prevention campaign. Called 46664 ("four-double-six six-four"), the campaign was named for his Robben Island prisoner number.

"When I told one of my advisors a few months ago that I wanted to retire, he growled at me: 'You are retired.' If that is really the case then I should say I now announce that I am retiring from retirement."

Nelson Mandela, June 1, 2004,
retirement speech

In 2004, just before his 86th birthday, Nelson announced his retirement from public life. "I do not intend to hide away totally from the public," he said to reporters, "but henceforth I want to be in the position of calling you to ask whether I would be welcome, rather than being called upon to do things and participate in events. The appeal therefore is: don't call me. I'll call you."

Two weeks later, Nelson carried the Olympic torch to Robben Island in the lead-up to the 2004 Summer Olympic Games in Athens, Greece. With stops in Cairo, Egypt, and Cape Town, South Africa, this was the first time in history that the Olympic torch relay had touched down in Africa.

On Nelson's 89th birthday, he founded a group called The Elders, an assembly of 12 senior leaders from around the world. Led by Archbishop Desmond Tutu, the group included a former leader of the United Nations, Kofi Annan, a former U.S. president, Jimmy Carter, and a former president of Ireland, Mary Robinson. The mission of the Elders was to use their collective wisdom to help solve global problems.

Nelson made his last-ever public appearance at the final match of the World Cup soccer tournament, held in Johannesburg in 2010. A year later, he met privately with U.S. First Lady Michelle Obama during her trip to South Africa.

By then, Nelson was very ill. He was in and out of the hospital with lung infections for the final three years of his life. He continued to divide his time between his homes in Qunu and Johannesburg until about a year before his

Nelson and his third wife, Graça Machel, visit Pollsmoor Prison in the late 1990s.

The village of Qunu as it looks today. This is where Nelson spent much of his youth, and it became a second home for him and his third wife, Graça, after he retired from politics in 1999. It also became his final resting place following his death in 2013.

death. At that point, he became so ill, he stayed in the city.

Nelson Mandela died at age 95 at his home in a suburb of Johannesburg on December 5, 2013. "Our nation has lost its greatest son," said South African President Jacob Zuma in announcing Nelson's passing. "What made Nelson Mandela great was precisely what made him human."

NELSON'S NAMES

Nelson Mandela was a man of many names, something that is customary in some African tribal cultures.

His given name was Rolihlahla, which in his native Xhosa language means "pulling the branch of a tree." In less formal usage, it can also mean "troublemaker."

Later, his name was changed to Nelson by a schoolteacher.

After his manhood ceremony, Nelson was also given a traditional name, Dalibunga, which means "one who creates dialogue," or "founder of the tribal council."

As he aged, Nelson was often called "Tata," the Xhosa word for "father."

The name that held the highest honor for Nelson was "Madiba." This was the name of Nelson's tribal clan, which was named after the founder of that clan. The original Madiba, Nelson's ancestor, was a Thembu chief who ruled in the 18th century.

Before Nelson's private funeral in Qunu, South Africa observed a 10-day period of mourning. For three days, his body lay in state (meaning his coffin was placed in a location where members of the public could pay their respects to him). Almost 100,000 people attended a public memorial, held in the stadium where Nelson had made his final public appearance. World leaders, members of royal families, celebrities, and sports stars joined the South African people in bidding farewell to Nelson. The world mourned because Nelson was, in the words of Britain's Prime Minister David Cameron, "a hero of our time."

Memories of Madiba

Such a short time since Nelson's death is too soon to fully understand what will be his long-term legacy in South Africa. Based on the depth of grief expressed by his country, and the rest

of the world, upon his passing, it is clear Nelson was a great man who made a great impact. He was someone who stood up for what he believed in, against all odds. He maintained his dignity, pride, and sense of humor, even when he was treated badly by others. His ability to forgive, and later work with, the people who oppressed him is a lesson for us all.

During his lifetime, Nelson was one of the most decorated people in history. Among hundreds of other honors, he holds 15 honorary citizenships in Europe, North America, and South America; at least 75 honorary degrees and fellowships from universities and colleges around the world; and 20 of the highest orders, knighthoods, and medals in the world. He is a Companion of the Order of Canada, and he was awarded the U.S. Presidential Medal of Freedom in 2002 by President George W. Bush. In addition, there are roads, gardens, student buildings, public squares, schools, sports centers, and parks around the world named for him. There are Mandela museums, sculptures, plaques, and statues. In 2009, the United Nations declared July 18, Nelson's birthday, as Mandela Day, an annual commemoration of his contributions to the world.

In 1993, *Time* magazine named Nelson as one of four Persons of the Year. A year later, the Johannesburg Press Club named him (along with former South African President F. W. de Klerk) as Newsmaker of the Year. At the turn of the century, Nelson's name was on many lists of influential and admired people of the 20th century. In 2006, Britain's *New Statesman* magazine listed Nelson as second in its list of

MANDELA IN THE MOVIES

The most recent film about Nelson Mandela opened in the United States about a week before Nelson died. Called *Long Walk to Freedom*, it is based on Nelson's 1994 autobiography. In that movie, British actor and rapper Idris Elba plays Nelson. Other famous actors who have portrayed him on screen are Danny Glover (1987), Sidney Poitier (1997), and Dennis Haysbert (2007). In 2009, Morgan Freeman played Nelson in the movie *Invictus*, about a famous rugby match, and in 2011, Terrence Howard played Nelson, while Jennifer Hudson portrayed the title character in the movie *Winnie Mandela*.

In addition to movies about Nelson, many musicians have written or dedicated songs to him. Stevie Wonder, Raffi, Nickelback, and Elvis Costello are the most famous musicians to pay musical tribute to Nelson.

Then-South African President F. W. de Klerk (seated, left) and soon-to-be-elected-President Nelson Mandela wait to speak in Philadelphia in 1993, the year that the two won the Nobel Peace Prize for their work in bringing about the transition from apartheid to democracy in South Africa.

A group of black and white boys playing soccer on a beach in South Africa in 2010, the year their country hosted soccer's World Cup. This simple photo is a tribute to the work and suffering of Nelson Mandela and those who struggled to help all Africans achieve freedom and equality.

50 Heroes of Our Time. (First place went to Burmese peace activist Aung San Suu Kyi.)

Despite all these honors, awards, and fellowships, Nelson was the first to admit he wasn't perfect, nor was he always the serene, forgiving, heroic character he became later in life. "I am not a saint," he often said, "unless you think of a saint as a sinner who keeps on trying."

The man who helped Nelson write his memoirs agrees. It was Nelson's years in prison that "formed the Mandela we know," wrote Richard Stengel after Nelson's death:

You Know You're Famous When ...

In 1973, British scientists named a newly discovered nuclear particle the "Mandela Particle," and, in 2004 and 2006, zoologists named two South African spiders after Nelson—*Stasimopus mandelai* (2004) and *Anelosimus nelsoni* (2006).

"The man who went into prison in 1962 was hotheaded and easily stung. The man who walked out into the sunshine of the mall in Cape Town 27 years later was measured, even serene.... In prison, he learned to control his anger. He had no choice. And he came to understand that if he was ever to achieve that free and nonracial South Africa of his dreams, he would have to come to terms with his oppressors. He would have to forgive them."

Today, Nelson Mandela is remembered by the world as a regal father figure, someone who put his nation and his beliefs before himself, a consensus builder who dedicated his life to making South Africa a respectful, inclusive nation for all who live there.

He helped bring democracy to one of the most divided nations in the world. He forgave the people who tried to crush him, even standing side by side with them for the sake of his country. He never stopped fighting for what he believed in, no matter what the cost.

He showed us that everyone—even a little boy from a tiny village that's just a speck on a map in the wilds of Africa—has a voice in this world.

Chronology

July 18, 1918 Rolihlahla Mandela born in Mvezo, South Africa.

1925 Rolihlahla starts school; teacher changes his name to Nelson.

1930 Nelson's father dies; Chief Jongintaba becomes his guardian.

1934 Takes part in a traditional ceremony that marks transition from boyhood to manhood; leaves home to start his studies at Clarkebury Boarding School.

1937 Moves to Healdtown, a British-style boarding school.

1939 Begins working toward a Bachelor of Arts degree at University of Fort Hare; meets Oliver Tambo.

1940 Is expelled from Fort Hare for protesting flawed student election.

1941 Runs away with adopted brother Justice to Johannesburg to escape arranged marriages; gets job as a clerk and messenger at law offices of Witkin, Sidelskly and Eidelman; meets Walter Sisulu.

1942 Starts attending meetings of African National Congress (ANC); Chief Jongintaba dies.

1943 Graduates from University of Fort Hare and begins studying law, part time, at University of the Witwatersrand; participates in first protest, a nine-day boycott of the Johannesburg bus system.

1944 Co-founds ANC Youth League; marries Evelyn Mase.

1946 Nelson and Evelyn's first son, Madiba Thembekile ("Thembi"), is born.

1947 First daughter, Makaziwe, is born; she dies nine months later.

1948 White National Party wins general election and forms government of South Africa; non-whites not allowed to vote in election; apartheid begins.

1950 Nelson and Evelyn's second son, Makgatho Lewanika, is born; ANC and other groups stage national day of protest, Freedom Day; police open fire on a crowd, killing 18 people.

1951 Nelson is elected president of the ANC Youth League.

1952 Defiance Campaign Against Unjust Laws begins; Nelson, one of its organizers, is arrested; serves two days in jail before judge gives him nine-month suspended sentence; he and friend Oliver Tambo create South Africa's first black law firm; government imposes its first banning order on Nelson; he is forbidden to attend meetings or to leave Johannesburg.

1953 Nelson and Evelyn's second daughter is born; they call her Makaziwe in honor of their first baby girl.

1955 Launches the Freedom Charter Campaign with other leaders; secretly attends the Congress of the People, where the Freedom Charter is read out to 3,000 people; Freedom Charter is adopted almost a year later; police raid Nelson's home; is arrested, along with 155 other prominent leaders; a month later, trial against those arrested begins.

1958 Divorces Evelyn and marries Nomzamo Winifred Madikizela ("Winnie"); a new, even more oppressive government takes power in South Africa; Grand Apartheid begins.

1959 Nelson and Winnie's first daughter, Zenani, is born.

1960 Nelson and Winnie's second daughter, Zindzi, is born; police kill 69 people in Sharpeville Massacre; nine days later, government declares a state of emergency; Nelson is arrested that day.

1961 Found not guilty in treason trial that began four years earlier; goes into hiding.

1961 Co-founds *Umkhonto we Sizwe* (MK), or "Spear of the Nation"; is Commander-in-Chief of this organization, which uses violent means to continue fight for freedom.

1962 Leaves South Africa; travels around Africa meeting supporters and learning warfare tactics; also visits London.

1962 Is arrested and charged with inciting, or convincing, workers to strike and leaving the country without a passport; is sentenced to five years in prison.

1963 While in prison, is also charged with sabotage and conspiracy; nine others are accused; their trial, called the "Rivonia Trial," begins.

1964 Takes the stand in the Rivonia Trial; delivers a speech, which becomes known as his "I Am Prepared To Die" speech; is sentenced to life in prison; taken to a maximum-security prison on Robben Island; becomes prisoner number 466/64.

1968 Mother dies of heart attack.

1969 Eldest son, Thembi, dies in car crash.

1975 Secretly begins writing life story; notes form basis for his autobiography, *Long Walk to Freedom,* which is published in 1994.

1976 Soweto Uprising draws international attention to the cruelty of South Africa's government.

1980 Oliver Tambo launches "Free Mandela" campaign, which spreads around the globe, making Nelson the most famous political prisoner in the world.

1982 Nelson is moved to Pollsmoor Prison after 18 years at Robben Island.

1985 South African President Botha offers to release Nelson if he will renounce violence as a tool to fight apartheid; Nelson refuses and instead writes a statement that his daughter Zindzi reads at a mass rally in Soweto.

1988 United Nations calls for Nelson's release; dozens of celebrities stage a massive concert for Nelson's 70th birthday.

1988 Is moved to private cottage on the grounds of Victor Verster Prison near Cape Town.

1989 F. W. de Klerk becomes president of South Africa.; he begins dismantling apartheid laws and frees many political prisoners.

1990 Nelson is released from prison.

1993 Nelson and de Klerk are jointly awarded Nobel Peace Prize.

1994 South Africa holds its first fully democratic election; Nelson votes for the first time in his life; becomes president of South Africa.

1996 Divorces Winnie.

1998 Marries Graça Machel.

1999 Retires from politics after one term as president.

2004 Announces retirement from public life.

2005 Son Makgatho dies of AIDS.

2010 Makes his last public appearance, at World Cup soccer finals.

December 5, 2013 Nelson Mandela dies at home, at age 95.

Glossary

appease To calm down by giving someone what he or she wants

bail Money given in a court case to allow the accused person to be free until the trial starts, but to ensure that he or she shows up for the trial; if the person doesn't show up, the court keeps the money

benefactor Someone who helps a person or group of people, often by giving money

birthright A right that a person or group of people automatically has because they were born in a certain place, or position

boycott To refuse to buy a product, use a service, or deal with a certain business or person, as a way to protest something; the goal is to convince the person or business to change something

charismatic Charming, attractive, or possessing other qualities that appeal to people

circumcision Surgery to remove the foreskin, or loose skin, covering the penis; usually done when the boy is still a baby

civil disobedience Refusal to obey a law, in a nonviolent manner, to protest something or to force a government to make change

consensus A group decision or opinion that everyone in the group agrees with

conspiracy A secret plot by more than one person to do something illegal or rebellious

correspondence course A program of study that allows students to do their schoolwork at home, rather than attending classes in person

corruption The misuse of power by a leader or government for illegal purposes or personal gain

curriculum A group of courses that make up an educational program

defiance Boldly resisting or challenging authority

demonstration A protest

dormitory A building that houses many people

hearings Court proceedings to determine one's innocence or guilt

honorary Given or granted as an honor, without having to fulfill usual requirements

inauguration An official ceremony where a new leader is sworn into public office

inclusive Not leaving out any person or group; including everyone concerned

liberation Freedom

mainstream Normal or conventional

makeshift A temporary substitute; something that will do in the absence of the real thing

manifesto A public declaration of beliefs, opinion, goals, or principles by an individual or group; it is often political in nature and sometimes includes a call for action or change

martial Relating to war, combat, or armed forces

on the lam In hiding, and on the run, from someone trying to capture you

oppressive (oppressor) Unjustly or cruelly controlling a person or group by those in a position of power; an oppressor is the person in control.

paramount Of the highest importance or authority; supreme

political prisoner A person put in jail because his or her belief system goes against that of the government

prestigious Impressive or important; held in high esteem

prosecutor In a court case, the lawyer who is trying to prove that the accused person is guilty

prospector A person who makes a living looking for gold, diamonds, or other riches in the earth

prosperous Wealthy

quarry An open pit where stones or other minerals are dug up

radicalism Supporting, or taking action to encourage, major social or political change; extremism

rebellious Disobedient or defiant; fighting against the rules or authority

reconciliation Bringing together individuals or groups who have conflicted with each other in the past

repressive Overly strict, often cruel or unjust; similar to oppressive

rite of passage A ceremony or event that marks a person's transition from one life stage to another

state of emergency A situation of natural disaster, war, or political unrest, during which a government may suspend its usual procedures and practices, including its citizens' rights and freedoms, in order to regain control.

strife Struggle, conflict; often violent or bitter

succumb To give up and give in to a great force, desire, or something you've been trying to fight off

testimony A person's statement or evidence presented in a court case

treason The betrayal of one's country

United Nations An international organization made up of most of the world's nations, founded in 1945 to promote global peace, security, and cooperation

warder A guard or warden

Further Information

Books

Brown, Laaren, and Lenny Hort. *Nelson Mandela: A Photographic Story of a Life.* New York: DK Publishing, 2006.

Kramer, Ann. *Nelson Mandela: From Political Prisoner to President.* Austin: Raintree Steck-Vaughn, 2003.

Nelson Mandela Foundation. *Nelson Mandela: The Authorized Comic Book*. New York: W.W. Norton, 2009.

Tames, Richard. *The End of Apartheid: A New South Africa*. Chicago: Heinemann Library, 2001.

Video/DVDs

Nelson Mandela's Life Story Documentary (online video). Nelson Mandela Foundation, 2012. Link for free viewing at: http://www.nelsonmandela.org/multimedia/entry/nelson-mandelas-life-story-documentary

Nelson Mandela: Son of Africa, Father of a Nation (DVD). Palm Pictures, 1996. Short preview online at: http://www.mandelasonofafrica.com/

The Five Lives of Nelson Mandela (online video). CNN, 2013. Two-minute tribute at: http://www.cnn.com/video/data/2.0/video/world/2013/12/05/five-lives-nelson-mandela-orig.cnn.html

Winnie Mandela (DVD). One Village, 2011.

Nelson Mandela: Life and Times (DVD). Kulture Video, 2010.

Mandela: Long Road to Freedom (DVD). Anchor Bay, 2013.

Websites

http://www.nelsonmandela.org/content/landing/life-times-of-nelson-mandela
On this site, titled *The Life and Times of Nelson Mandela,* you can read Nelson's biography, view an interactive timeline of his life, or search databases full of audio clips, videos, photos and books about Nelson. The FAQ section will answer all your questions.

http://www.biography.com/people/nelson-mandela-9397017
On this site, you will find a full biography of Nelson Mandela, photo collections, and a series of short videos about his life.

http://www.mandela.gov.za/index.html
This excellent, well-organized site may be the most complete source of information about Nelson Mandela. It includes a lovely section of tributes to Nelson by other world leaders, transcripts of his speeches since 1951, links, quotes, photos, videos, FAQs, and more.

http://archive.nelsonmandela.org/home?view=gallery
The Nelson Mandela Digital Archive Project is an amazing multi-media presentation of various stages of Nelson's life. Under the section titled "Nelson Mandela and Young People," you can watch video segments of *Nelson Mandela: The Authorized Comic Book.*

https://www.youtube.com/watch?v=AgcTvoWjZJU
This music video of "Free Nelson Mandela," by the Specials, a British ska/reggae band, was produced in 1984 and became an anthem for the "Free Mandela" campaign in South Africa and around the world. Featuring an irresistible beat, haunting melody and lyrics, and lively dance performances, it draws upon a variety of musical influences from South Africa. The popular song delivers its message of protest against the apartheid policies of the South African government in an upbeat, celebratory style.

Index

About the Author

Diane Dakers was born and raised in Toronto, and now makes her home in Victoria, British Columbia. A specialist in Canadian arts and cultural issues, Diane has been a newspaper, magazine, television and radio journalist since 1991. She loves finding and telling stories about what makes people tick—be they world-changers like Nelson Mandela, or lesser-known folks like you and me.